Jekyll and

A Play

Leonard H. Caddy

Samuel French – London
New York – Sydney – Toronto – Hollywood

CHARACTERS

Poole, the butler
Charlotte, a maid
Dr Henry Jekyll who becomes **Mr Edward Hyde**
Celestine
Dr Lanyon, her uncle
Utterson, a lawyer
Hilda, the parlour maid
Penny, Hyde's woman
Child

The action takes place in the parlour and part of the adjoining laboratory in Dr Jekyll's house in London

Time—1851

PRODUCTION NOTES

It is assumed that Jekyll's transformations into Hyde will be achieved by alteration of stance, movement, expression and voice on the part of the actor, and by such changes as removing trim moustache from Jekyll, adding ugly projecting false teeth for Hyde, and a change from neat Jekyll hair to Hyde's unruly tangle by removing or adding a wig (or by the actor ruffling his own hair if this looks more effective). Some over-dressing by Jekyll such as a false cravat and stiff collar on a spring neckband to cover Hyde's untidy and dirty neckwear should be employed. The changes should become progressively more marked, the later ones being abetted by adding make-up and dirty, ragged clothing. The actor could use a mask if this is felt to be more effective. The techniques employed in effecting the transformations are envisaged as follows:

Scene 1   The make-up, wig, teeth etc. required for the transformation should be set ready for Jekyll behind the armchair, so that when he slumps behind it, he can quickly effect the change to Hyde.

Scene 2   The transformation can be made off stage.

Scene 3   Jekyll changes into Hyde while crouched behind the table, concealed by the chenille tablecloth, under which the make-up has been set.

Scene 4   The transformation can be made off stage.

Scene 5   The make-up should be set by the armchair in the laboratory, so that Jekyll can effect the transformation concealed by the armchair while the laboratory is in darkness.

ACT 1

SCENE 1

The parlour and part of the adjoining laboratory in Dr Jekyll's house. Early on a summer's evening. 1851

The parlour is a sombre room. It has a masculine appearance with evidence of the owner's medical calling. There is a table surrounded by several upright chairs C and an armchair by the fireplace LC. To one side of the fireplace there is a servants' bell and a sideboard. In the back wall there is a window UL and a bureau. There is a door DL to the hall and another R to the laboratory, with a bookcase next to it. The part of the laboratory that can be seen is dark, dingy and cold. An old armchair with its back to the audience, a stool, part of a workbench and a cabinet is all that can be seen. Other furniture may be added to complete the period décor at the discretion of the director

When the CURTAIN *rises, the door to the laboratory is open and a tuneless singing can be heard off R*

> *Poole enters the parlour from the hall and goes to the sideboard, instinctively checking for dust as he goes. He unlocks the tantalus and is about to confirm that the level of liquid is unaltered when he becomes aware of the singing and its source. He marches grimly into the laboratory and exits. There is a squeal, off, and Poole reappears leading Charlotte by the ear. She is carrying a duster and wears a white apron that is noticeably too large for her, and although her ear obviously hurts, she would never dare complain. They move into the parlour, and Poole locks the laboratory*

Poole And what do you think you are doing in there?
Charlotte Dusting, like you said.

Poole cuffs her round the ear

Mr Poole, sir. (*She automatically bobs as she speaks*)
Poole (*putting the key in the bureau*) How did you get in?
Charlotte Through the door—it was open—Mr Poole, sir. (*She bobs*)
Poole That door is never open. Nobody goes in there, not even me. Even a wretch like you knows that.
Charlotte How can I know? I've never been up to this part of the house before . . .
Poole And you will never come into it again, the scullery is where you belong—or the gutter. Get out.
Charlotte But the doctor said I was to do the parlour while Hilda was bad. Mr Poole, sir.
Poole (*coldly*) And I say get out.

He is about to give her another cuff when voices are heard off. He opens the door DL to bustle Charlotte out but realizes it is too late and so stands her in a corner by the door

Say one word and you will suffer. Good evening, sir.

Dr Jekyll enters

Charlotte bobs as he passes her

Jekyll Trouble, Poole?

Poole Nothing that need concern you, sir.

Jekyll (*turning back towards the door*) Come along in, my dear. (*To Poole*) The Madeira I think.

Celestine enters, followed by her uncle Dr Lanyon and Mr Utterson, an elderly lawyer

Charlotte contrives to bob a curtsy to each as they pass, and to be safe, repeats the practice whenever any of them come near her

Poole Good evening, madam. Doctor. Sir. (*He moves to the sideboard and begins to pour drinks*)

Celestine The house is very pleasant, Henry; although this room is far from pretty. It calls for more colour.

Jekyll It is a man's room.

Utterson sits in the armchair by the fireplace

Celestine (*crossing to the door of the laboratory*) And this must be the laboratory—oh, it's locked. I enjoyed our walk, Henry. Some of the squares we saw were most delightful. I cannot recall how long it is since I have walked so far. (*She moves towards the table*)

Utterson rises from the armchair, but Celestine declines his offer

(*Perching on one of the upright chairs*) Thank you—this will suffice.

Utterson takes a glass of wine from the tray Poole is preparing and sits again

(*To Jekyll*) Why do you keep your laboratory locked?

Jekyll There are compounds and mixes that could prove dangerous, they are better locked.

Lanyon Medicine is not like it used to be in your father's day, dear. Those cruel days are past, medicine is taking its place as an exact science.

Utterson An inexact science I should say, by the number of times it changes its mind.

Poole serves the wine. Utterson puts his empty glass on the tray as it passes. Poole refills it for him

Lanyon The body is a marvellous machine and we are learning more about it every day. A living machine and we are the engineers.

Jekyll I refuse to be drawn. Over the port next Friday, but not this afternoon. (*To Celestine*) Excuse us, won't you?

Celestine Quite all right, Henry. I know how much my uncle looks forward to your regular discussions—that and the Sunday morning sermon are his only real pleasures in life. Though what I cannot understand is if you are both physicians how it is that you differ so.

Lanyon Henry just will not accept that God made us all and he made each part of all of us—and what God made so we are. Harvey opened the door for us. It's quite clear, the liver, the gall, the spleen—*(he remembers there is a lady present)*—all our various parts, including our brain!—are all linked to make one whole body, destined to follow God's decree.

Celestine Are we then just animals?

Lanyon No. God gave us a soul.

Jekyll He gave us a brain, Lanyon. A brain that is capable of realizing that there is such a thing as a soul.

Utterson A brain that is capable of realizing that there is such a thing as a God.

Jekyll *(without having to look)* Mr Utterson's glass must be empty, Poole.

Poole refills Utterson's glass. The others decline more

(To Lanyon) My dear stick-in-the-mud, when my investigations are complete . . .

Lanyon When they are complete! This last idea of yours has been going on for months, it never will be complete, it cannot be complete—because it won't work.

Jekyll When my investigations are complete it will provide the proof that within the brain is locked everything that has ever happened to us and every emotion that we have ever felt, whether we expressed them or not.

Lanyon Bunkum, sir.

Celestine Uncle!

Jekyll The brain is not part of the body—the body is part of the brain and fundamentally entirely under its control.

Lanyon That is blasphemy, Henry.

Celestine Not so serious, Henry. I must leave for Scotland tomorrow, argue with Uncle when I am gone.

There is a slight pause. Celestine, glass in hand, rises and wanders DL. Charlotte, who has been standing still, silent and forgotten, bobs to her as she passes

Why is this child trying to imitate the monkey on the hurdy-gurdy man's barrow? *(To Jekyll)* She's not the parlour maid, is she?

Jekyll For today I believe she is—Poole?

Poole Just for today, sir. We have four girls down with the fever, madam. Tomorrow, sir . . .

Lanyon Ah, the Summer Ague: the blood becomes overheated in the sun you know.

Utterson This is the first fine day we have had for a week.

Celestine *(to Charlotte)* So you are Dr Jekyll's parlour maid.

Poole is about to deny any responsibility but she stops him

For today.

Charlotte mouths inaudibly and bobs yet another curtsy

And what is your name?

Her nervousness increasing to fear, Charlotte looks to Poole for instruction. He signifies that she must answer but is fearful of the result. She swallows and answers but no sound emerges—her second attempt is successful but unduly loud

Charlotte (*in a rush*) Charlotteifitpleaseyouma'am. (*Then more successfully*) Charlotte if it please you, ma'am.

Celestine Then as parlour maid should you not be helping Mr Poole by clearing the glasses?

Poole resignedly indicates that she should proceed. She stuffs the duster in her apron pocket, and with painful care, takes the tray and begins to gather the empty glasses

I find this interesting, I have very little experience of male society; tell me, is all masculine talk so dull?

Utterson It seems to be in this house. To my certain knowledge these two have had precisely the same conversation every Friday for seven years.

Lanyon Henry is obsessed with the importance of the brain—

Charlotte, overawed to the point of terror, hovers near Celestine who still holds her glass

Celestine Don't just stand there girl—take it.

She thrusts her glass into Charlotte's hand causing her to all but upset the tray. Charlotte with painful care slowly carries the tray round behind them under the unflinching eye of Poole

Lanyon —he seems to think that any brain is capable of learning anything—and that each one has just as much potential as the next.

Jekyll Lanyon . . .

Celestine Do you mean that quality and breeding mean nothing, Henry?

Jekyll I mean that it is the brain that learns everything, from how to talk—how to breathe even, up to how to—create the power of the steam engine or how to write a great symphony.

Lanyon Or how to understand the will of the Almighty.

Jekyll It generates the desires and dictates the emotions—it is capable of learning anything—even of how to control its own creations. Who knows what is locked up inside the brain because it has learned it is not permitted to let it out. Who knows? God's greatest gift to man is a brain—of infinite capacity.

Celestine I refuse to accept that all intellects are equal.

Jekyll The capacity of the brain of an ignorant uneducated crossing man is forty-nine and a half ounces. And the capacity of my brain is forty-nine and a half ounces. The brain of . . .

Utterson The Archbishop of Canterbury.

Jekyll Name who you will. Within very close limits—forty-nine and a half ounces. Each has an equal amount of cerebelite, the chemical structure of

each is identical. In every aspect indistinguishable. Therefore given the right
conditions each must be equally capable.

Lanyon Of course the brain of a woman is smaller, bound to be; they all
measure—how much did you say the average was Henry?

Jekyll Almost without exception between forty-three and forty-five ounces.

Charlotte stands by the sideboard, enthralled by her surroundings

Celestine Henry. I cannot let this pass. The fact that the brain of a woman
is smaller than that of a man I accept; that is as I would expect it to be. But
for you to suggest that my brain is in no way different from *(she points
to Charlotte)*—that pathetic creature's I find intolerable.

*To be the sudden centre of attention is too much for Charlotte. She suddenly
realizes that she still holds the tray and hurriedly puts it down on the sideboard
with a loud clatter. She stands transfixed*

Come here girl. Come here, I say. You see she has not even the intellect
to obey a simple command like that. *(She turns away)*

*Poole lands a surreptitious swipe on Charlotte and hisses at her to obey. Jekyll
moves across to them*

Jekyll *(with gentle firmness)* Do as the lady says, Charlotte.

Charlotte moves slowly to Celestine

(Aside to Poole) Cuff her by all means Poole, but not when there are ladies
in the room.

Poole I'm sorry, sir.

*Charlotte stands beside Celestine in mounting embarrassment, fear and dis-
appointment*

Celestine Now Henry. *(To Charlotte)* Stand here, girl. Not too close. Look
at us both and tell me again that there is no difference in our intellects.

Jekyll What I said, my dear, was that in size, composition and structure there
is very little difference if any in your brains. There is no physical reason
why the brain inside this poor creature's head should not be just as capable
as your own of dexterity—or imagination—or emotion.

Utterson *(aloud but unnoticed)* Probably more capable.

Lanyon I think you go too far some times.

Jekyll But you see, your brain has learned its responsibilities, it has acquired
the right qualities and completely restrained anything undesirable. This one
has learned to repress expression—even to repress the ability to learn. Of
course when I use the word "learn", I do not mean learn as a discipline of
acquiring facts from a *maître* or tutor, or even from some wretched school-
master. I mean what is known as the "learning of nature"; for instance no-
one teaches—no-one can teach—the ability to feel happy or sad, or to be
kind or cruel. These we learn from nature. A baby has learned to laugh
and cry before it has been taught to speak.

Lanyon Ah, but once you have taught it to speak you can soon teach it not
to cry.

Jekyll You cannot teach it not to *want* to cry.

The two men are clearly heading for another long discussion

Celestine Gentlemen. No, there is no need to apologize, Henry. But there is one element you have completely omitted from your argument. Quality! It is not a case of learning, it is a case of breeding. In our family we can count two baronets and even connections with a duke. Whereas this child . . . If you say our brains are the same size, then incredible as I may find it, I will accept the fact. But of the same quality—no. It could as well be said there was the same amount of material in a length of French brocade as there is in a length of rough weave. Well there is. But you must admit that the quality is not comparable. (*She stops, satisfied with her own argument*)

There is a slight pause

Lanyon I fear we have bored you with our debate, my dear.
Celestine Not at all, I found it most stimulating. Indeed I feel I may have been able to add an aspect that you may otherwise have overlooked.
Jekyll (*to Lanyon*) We must go into the difference between "want" and "learn" on Friday, my friend.

Celestine directs her attention to Charlotte, who is now embarrassed almost beyond control

Celestine Well girl, and what have you done with this brain of yours?

Charlotte does not understand

Have you ever had lessons or instructions?
Charlotte The reverend gen'leman taught us letters and numbers at the House, ma'am.

It is Celestine who does not understand this time

Celestine The "House"?
Jekyll She must be one of the Graycape girls we have taken in; from the orphanage up at—(*He looks at Poole*)
Poole Wapping, sir. (*To Celestine over the head of Charlotte*) I have an understanding with the mistress of the Institute, ma'am. When we have need of a girl below stairs we take one of the older Graycapes and give them a place. They seldom prove a success though.
Jekyll Thank you, Poole.
Celestine (*to Jekyll*) That is very commendable of you. I am glad you are not old-fashioned in your attitude to the poor. It is up to us to help them cope with their position. When I think how our forebears regarded them I am sometimes quite ashamed. They seem to treat them more like animals. Do you not agree, Mr Utterson?
Utterson According to Darwin we are all animals.
Celestine (*not understanding this remark*) Yes. (*She returns her attention to Charlotte*) Strange how the poor display good features sometimes. This girl for instance has really a quite well-formed bone structure about the cheek and the brow. Could well come from someone of far better standing.

Utterson Very likely did.
Celestine Really, sir. I can never decide whether you are being profound or profane.
Utterson I apologize my dear lady, I will try to be more succinct in future.
Jekyll Pay him no heed, you are not yet accustomed to Utterson's ways. He can be rude, outspoken, morose—
Lanyon Downright blasphemous sometimes.
Jekyll—sarcastic and cutting. But he is excellent company and can pick a flaw in an argument quicker than any man I know.

Charlotte begins to sob—despite all efforts, she can no longer control her emotions; the others turn to look at her and her feelings start to overflow through her increasing tears

Charlotte It's not my fault—can't help it—didn't want to go to no orphanage—didn't ask to be a Graycape.

Poole is about to take physical action but checks himself. The others are too affronted, surprised or interested to take action

Never had no help, always had to do what I'm told. I try but I always do it wrong. Not my fault. (*Now quite oblivious of her position her feelings pour forth, possibly for the first time in her life. She turns to Celestine*) Don't blame me if my face ain't right, didn't ask for it to be like this. Anyway I never seen what my face was like 'til I came here to Doctor's house. And don't blame me if I don't know anything—'cause I ain't never been taught anything. The only thing I've been told is what I do wrong. Why ain't it fair? (*For a moment her tears get the better of her*)

The outrage and retribution of the others is stopped by Jekyll. He dismisses the furious Poole

Poole exits

Jekyll signals the other men not to interfere and settles the outraged Celestine in a chair. He is clearly fascinated by this development

(*More calmly, as if to herself*) I do what I am told—I always do what I am told—I try to be a good girl. If I was told more I'd know more. (*To Celestine*) If I'd been told as much as you have I'd know as much as you do. And be as clever, Doctor said so; I heard him—he said I'm the same as you are really it's only . . . He said I was as good as you are . . . He said . . . as good as you are . . . He . . .

What she has done dawns on her and she stops. Realizing the awfulness of her position, she lets out a long dreadful sob and stumbles from the room

There is a pause and then everybody speaks at once, ad libbing. Celestine is so insulted that she doesn't know whether she is going to faint or not; Lanyon, also affronted, tries to tell Jekyll so and attend to his niece at the same time; Jekyll is keenly excited—he tells Utterson to see that Poole does not harm the girl

Utterson exits

Celestine Henry. How could you let her. After all you have done for her.
Jekyll (*pouring a glass of wine*) She spoke straight out without any restraint at all.
Celestine I shall never forget it as long as I live.

Jekyll offers her the wine

No thank you.

Jekyll puts the glass on the table

I have never been so insulted. There is no other word for it.
Lanyon Never heard anything like it in my whole life.
Celestine If only I was a man I would know what to do about it.
Lanyon A servant and an orphan at that.

Jekyll begins to pace about excitedly behind them

Celestine To think I should ever be spoken to . . . and after I had been so pleasant to her; that is what is so unbearable. You try to treat them like human beings and—this happens.
Lanyon Never in my whole life . . .
Celestine You will punish her before she goes of course, Henry.

Jekyll stops pacing

For her own sake—we must help her learn. How will you do it?

Utterson enters

Jekyll looks at him, but he only shrugs, then takes the glass of wine from the table and settles in his usual chair. The others look at Jekyll, who is still alive with excitement. To their surprise, he lets out a sharp laugh of delight

Jekyll Hah! Hah! That was absolutely splendid.
Celestine Henry?
Lanyon Don't follow you, old man.
Jekyll Don't you see? (*He paces about*) It's another proof of my theory. That girl, what sort of person was she?
Celestine Crude, ill-bred and in need of a whipping.
Lanyon Not a very intelligent specimen I would say.
Utterson Damned unlucky.
Jekyll Exactly. She *is* ill-bred, unintelligent and possibly in need of a whipping; but that is what life has made of her—that is what *we* have made of her. What is she like underneath all that? What is she really like? I'll tell you. She is of great intellect and considerable dignity.

The others protest in amazement

Lanyon We shall soon have to be going . . .
Jekyll (*indifferent to all else*) She understood. She stood there in a strange world and she understood. That pathetic wretch, who has possibly never heard any language other than back-stairs tattle and orphanage cant, knew what I was talking about. It's a wonderful confirmation of my theory.

Celestine How deranged ranting can confirm any theory I just do not comprehend.

There is a slight pause

Jekyll Deep inside us is the person we really are. It is buried by what life has made us; where we were born, how we were tutored: as life goes on it gets deeper and deeper—but it is always there.

Celestine *(quietly)* Sounds horrible.

Jekyll *(ignoring her)* It is a false face we put to the world forever hiding what we really are. But just now with that poor child it happened: social fear, which must have been awful to her, was so strong that it broke through this false face and just for a moment—a fleeting moment—we saw a flash of the real person. A person of superior intellect and, if my surmise is correct, of considerable charm.

Lanyon I refuse to accept that demented outburst as any sort of proof of your theory of compound personality. Anyway we must be going, we only called in for a moment, it will soon be dark and I have no intention of Celestine ...

Celestine One moment please, Uncle. *(To Jekyll)* I know you are very clever and that you lecture at the Royal Institute, but are you seriously suggesting that—inside me I am somebody quite different? Even somebody who might be—well not quite nice?

Jekyll I am not suggesting it, my dear; I am stating it as a fact. Not that you are "not quite nice"—but that none of us know what we really are. The inner reality fascinates me.

Celestine All I can say is that I am glad we can never know. What is buried can stay buried; I will be content to be what I am.

Utterson Most of us are.

Jekyll *(almost to himself)* That child must have been quite terrified. I wonder if fear is the key.

Lanyon and Celestine move towards the door

Lanyon Well Henry, we'll sort this out on Friday shall we, eh? Usual time?

Jekyll Eh? Of course, please forgive me. Let me see, your hat, your gloves.

Lanyon In the hall—downstairs.

Jekyll Let me send a man round to the Livery for a carriage for you.

Celestine By no means. After the excitement of the last hour I feel in need of some air, I shall benefit from the walk.

Utterson rises

Jekyll You off too, Utterson? Another glass before you go.

Utterson sits again

Celestine I shall look forward to our meeting again, Henry; I did so enjoy my first visit to your house, although I trust that any further call on my part will prove to be of a more restful nature.

Jekyll I promise. Next time you visit your uncle I shall have a dinner especially for you. I shall invite some ladies to keep you company and the conversation shall be of nothing but clothes and music. (*He opens the door*)

Celestine (*as she exits*) I shall have a new gown made for the occasion. I have a length of green brocade that will do admirably . . .

She exits

Lanyon A dinner party, Henry? With ladies in the company—who the deuce will you invite? You don't know any ladies . . .

He exits

Jekyll No I don't, do I. I'd quite forgotten that.

He exits, closing the door behind him

Utterson rises and pours himself another glass of wine, He takes a cigar from his pocket and trims the end in the fireplace. The Lights begin to fade very slowly, as dusk falls. Utterson stands deep in thought. The silence is broken by a gentle tap at the door, followed a moment later by another tap

Utterson Come.

The door slowly opens and Charlotte enters fearfully

Well.

Charlotte Oh, it's you, sir. I thought the doctor was here. Sorry, sir.

Utterson Don't start crying again, girl, you have done enough of that for one day. Where have you been hiding?

Charlotte In the big cupboard on the back landing, sir. I didn't know what to do. I'd been so bad in front of the doctor, now Mr Poole will throw me out—and I've got nowhere to go—I can't go back to the House.

Utterson watches her in silence

Sir, do you think if I asked him, the doctor would let me stay the night; see—give me a better chance. Would he, do you think?

Utterson still says nothing, but his face is beginning to show kindness—a rare expression for this stern old face

Sir, can I ask you something—please. (*She pauses*) I know I shouldn't ask you this but in my whole life I have never had a gentleman talk to me like you are. (*She pauses again*) I like you.

Utterson nearly smiles

Sir, please, would you ask him for me? If I can stay—just for tonight—sir. I think you'd be able to put it better than me. Didn't last long as a parlour maid, did I? Will you ask him, sir? Will he let me do you think?

Utterson (*after a pause*) Intellect and charm, damn it.

Charlotte Beg pardon, sir?

Utterson We'll ask him together. I think he will let you stay.

Charlotte Thank you, sir. (*She all but gives him a hug*)

Jekyll enters briskly

Charlotte retreats to a respectful distance in the shadows

Jekyll Well, well, well. Ladies are pleasant enough creatures to have about the place occasionally—but you cannot really relax until they have left you to your own devices, can you? Now then a glass of wine, you'll not refuse? (*He goes to the sideboard*)

Utterson I seldom do.

Jekyll Damn it, the Madeira's all gone, I'll ring for some more. Or will you settle for claret—or perhaps brandy?

Utterson I'd settle for gin if it was all that you had.

Jekyll Claret?

Utterson Whichever is the fuller.

Jekyll Claret. (*He pours two drinks and gives one to Utterson*) Interesting afternoon I think. (*He rings the bell and then sits down at the table*) From my point of view that outburst was very significant—poor Celestine was most put out.

Utterson clears his throat

(*Looking around*) What's the matter? Who's there? (*He sees Charlotte*) Oh, it's you. Where have you been hiding yourself?

Utterson Amongst the sheets apparently.

Jekyll Come here, let's have a look at you.

Charlotte goes to him

She was right, it is a well-formed brow. Who were your parents, child?

Charlotte Don't know, sir.

Jekyll Neither of them?

She shakes her head. Jekyll's manner suddenly changes

(*With convincing brutality*) What would you do if I were to hit you good and hard? (*He gives every indication that he is going to do just that*)

Charlotte (*cowering in fear but not moving*) Nothing, sir.

Jekyll (*relaxing to normal*) No—nothing. (*To Utterson*) You see, a frightened animal again. But we know there is another spirit there, don't we. One day, Utterson, I shall be able to release it—find out what lies beneath.

There is a tap on the door and Poole enters. His benign expression changes to fury as he sees Charlotte

Ah, Poole. See to the Madeira will you.

Poole Very good, sir.

Jekyll And take . . . (*He looks at Charlotte*)

Charlotte Charlotte, sir.

Jekyll Charlotte downstairs. There must be something for her to be getting on with 'til bedtime.

Poole There is, sir, plenty. (*He takes the empty decanter from the sideboard*)

Charlotte hesitates

Jekyll Get along with you. You must work to earn your keep.

Charlotte looks at him, as if to speak, then looks at Utterson

What is it girl?

Charlotte Nothing, sir—good-night, sir. (*To Utterson*) Good-night, sir. And thank you, sir.

Poole bustles her towards the door

Jekyll Oh Poole. I am expecting a delivery from Campion the chemist people, has it arrived yet?

Poole Not yet, sir.

Jekyll Let me know the moment it does.

Poole Very good, sir.

Poole and Charlotte exit. The door closes, and there is the muffled sound of a slap and a squeal, off

Utterson (*after a pause*) You keeping her on? The little brat—keeping her on?

Jekyll Don't see why not. (*Chuckling*) Of course I will have to keep her out of sight when Celestine calls.

Utterson She didn't realize it but she came back to apologize to you, you know. Funny little urchin.

There is a pause

Jekyll Utterson, should a man marry do you think? Cannot help thinking that a man in my position would benefit from having a wife about the place sometimes. I'm forty now you know. Seems a right sort of age. What do you think?

Utterson Don't know what to think—never have known what to think about women. That is why I have never married I suppose. Didn't know you were even interested in the creatures.

Jekyll In my younger days—oh yes. My first years at Oxford I was quite a roué.

Utterson You surprise me.

Jekyll That is all so deeply buried in the past that I have forgotten all about it now. I must have been a different person—incredible. No, a respectable marriage to someone of standing, someone who can take her place beside me at functions and talk intelligently; would be a great advantage to life, I cannot help feeling.

Utterson Someone like Lanyon's young niece.

Jekyll Why not? She seems to fit the bill admirably and during her visit we have met several times; I feel I could become quite fond of her in time.

Utterson That would seem to be an advantage if you intend to marry the girl.

They sit in silence for a moment

What about your work?

Jekyll That would go on, naturally. No, I couldn't consider marriage until my present investigations are complete. Once I have established my

principle and written my definitive article, then I will settle down and
marry and work for the good of—well, anybody who needs it.

There is a pause as they sip their wine

Utterson It wouldn't do any good to suggest that you just settle down and
marry and not pursue your research.
Jekyll (*rising*) It would not.
Utterson Didn't think it would. Is it dangerous?
Jekyll I don't know. I am beginning to think that fear or fright of some kind
is involved.
Utterson I don't like it. Take the advice of an old fool who has spent most
of his life in that mean midden called a court of law, and seen most of the
nastiness that we humans create for ourselves. There is enough fear in the
world, Henry—it's wrong somewhere. Use your powers in some other
way.
Jekyll Not you too, Utterson. You are not going to tell me that my work
is an affront to God, are you? God made us, all I want to do is find out
what he made before we humans altered it and moulded it. Surely it is man's
duty to find out what he is really like. You have never questioned ethics
before—why now?
Utterson I do not question your ethics, Henry. I do not concern myself with
God; he is competent to look after himself I have no doubt. It's not God
I base my advice to you on—it's the Devil! I see it every day, shallow or
deep, there is a Devil buried in every man. Give it up.

There is no answer

I have talked too much. I have either had too much wine or not enough.
(*He rises*) Besides Mrs Camp extracted a promise from me that I would not
be late for supper tonight. She has a venison hock or some such thing—
and as the appointed hour has already passed by a quarter I feel I should
take my leave in deference to the aforementioned joint and the impending
strain of relationship between master and housekeeper. Until Friday.

There is a knock at the door and Poole enters with a small package

Poole Excuse me, sir, but the boy has just brought this and you did say...
Jekyll (*taking the package and opening it*) Ah thank you Poole. Yes, this looks
about right. Oh, Poole, Mr Utterson was just leaving; see him to the door,
would you? And then see that I am not disturbed.
Utterson Is that stuff dangerous?
Jekyll There is enough here to poison the whole household.
Utterson What are you going to do with it? Part of your compound I suppose.
Jekyll Part of the key to the hidden man, Utterson—part of the key.
Utterson This fellow you are making these tests on—it's not likely to do him
any real harm is it?
Jekyll Who?
Utterson This fellow down at—where is it? Bartholomew's Infirmary. The one
you try all these mixtures out on.

Jekyll Oh. I see what you mean. No, I assure you, I am most particular, there is no danger. I had forgotten I had told you about that. That's it—he is afflicted with the paralysis poor fellow, there is little he can do in the world— seems quite pleased to be able to help. That's it. Hyde his name is—Edward Hyde.

Utterson What do you do? Give him some stuff and then just watch him all night? Anyway, you know best. You know my views—good-night, Henry. Give my regards to the Devil when you meet him.

Utterson exits, followed by Poole

Jekyll Give my regards to the Devil indeed. (*Peering at his pocket-watch*) Now then, eight o'clock. The social niceties are finished for the day—we can start work. (*Happy and eager to be at his work, he takes the key from the bureau and unlocks the laboratory door. He moves back to the table and picks up the package. He sees the unfinished glass of wine*) Pity to waste good claret. (*He raises the glass*) A toast. A toast to me. May Henry Jekyll be a wiser man come the dawn. (*He drinks but chokes a little on it and coughs*) Dear me, that's not a very good start. (*He puts the glass on the sideboard, takes a box of matches from the mantelpiece and goes into the laboratory. He strikes a match by the bench*) Damn it, of all the confounded incompetence. (*He sweeps back into the parlour and across to the door DL*) Servants. (*Opening the door*) Poole! What the Hades happened to the lamp in the laboratory? (*He shuts the door and stands in frustration*) I must find out tonight. I'll work in here. Must get on. (*He goes into the laboratory and takes a wooden carrying case from the bench. He brings the case and the package of chemical into the parlour, placing them on the table. He prepares to light the lamp*)

A rather breathless Poole enters

There is oil all over the bench in there, Poole!

Poole (*taking the match*) Allow me, sir. (*He lights the lamp which throws a circle of light in a small area around the table*) Oil, sir, I don't understand.

Jekyll goes into the laboratory and collects phials, measuring glasses, tweezers, mixing rods, dishes etc.

Jekyll Oil, damn it! Oil. (*He brings the apparatus into the parlour and arranges it on the table*) The place is like a candle-works on a hot day.

Poole I'll have it cleared immediately, sir.

Jekyll (*going into the laboratory again*) You'll do no such thing. I will sort it out in the morning. Is there any water in there?

Poole Yes, sir.

Jekyll Is it clean?

Poole Naturally, sir.

Jekyll (*coming into the parlour and locking the laboratory door behind him*) Put it on the table then. (*He busies himself arranging the apparatus*)

Poole takes the jug of water from the sideboard and places it on the table. He draws the window curtains

I've just remembered, I failed to put that lamp out to be filled this morning. Who filled it? (*Sternly*) Did you? Did you go in there?
Poole I did not, sir.
Jekyll Somebody over-filled it and left the wick trailing.
Poole Just before you returned from your promenade, sir, I discovered that wretched little Graycape messing about in there.
Jekyll In there?
Poole Said she was dusting, sir. I reprimanded . . .
Jekyll But she wouldn't know how to begin to fill a lamp of that sort.
Poole Apparently not, sir.
Jekyll (*relaxing*) Confound it, she had a deucedly good try, she all but succeeded. (*He is almost laughing*)
Poole I will deal with her, sir. I think a night in the outside coal cellar and then dismissal.
Jekyll Why does everybody want to get rid of the poor little thing? (*More seriously*) You will send her to bed, Poole, as with the rest of the staff. You will then retire yourself. I have work to do and I must under no circumstances be disturbed. This house must be locked up and abed within one quarter of an hour. Do you understand?
Poole Clearly, sir. (*Moving to the door*) Good-night, sir.

Jekyll, busy at the table, does not answer

Poole exits

Jekyll goes to the bureau, unlocks a drawer and takes out a notebook. He returns to the table with his notes, a pen and a bottle of ink. Sitting, he looks through his notes

Jekyll (*reading as he turns the pages*) "Compound seven . . . dizziness." Ha, we have progressed since then. (*Reading*) "Item thirty-one . . . violent sickness . . ." I remember poor Lanyon thought I was going to die, he was convinced I had fluid on the lung. If only he had known. (*Returning to his notes*) "Item ninety-eight . . . must be on the threshold of success." Huh, how many times have I written that? Now, last night's entry. (*Reading*) "Item ninety-nine. Results of breakdown of brain filament from cadaver. Negative apart from number seven which showed some softening." And what was number seven? "Foulton's Asthmatic Compound." No wonder I underlined it; of all things, a quack remedy from the streets. Whatever made me try it in the first place? But it definitely reacted on the filament. Mixed with my own compound . . . must be . . . must be . . . (*He sits silently for a moment*) And what did Mr Foulton's elixir prove to be? (*Reading*) "Ninety parts water, nine parts honey and one part . . ." (*He takes up the package and looks at it*) A concentrated extract from the bark of the humble willow tree. Now we have Mr Foulton's secret we can proceed. (*He picks up the pen. As he writes*) "Item one hundred. Procedure. One: confirm that brain filament does soften in—" let's call it "—Foulton's Mixture. Two: add Foulton's Mixture to own compound. Three: test." If only it were as simple as it sounded. (*He carefully takes a phial of crystals from the package, empties* *the contents into a bottle, adds water and mixes*) A concentrate of Foulton's Mixture. (*He pours a small amount of the mixture into a dish, takes a jar from the carrying box and extracts a small strip of intangible matter from it with tweezers*) Procedure: confirm that brain filament softens in Foulton's Mixture. Brain filament. (*Picking up the dish*) Foulton's Mixture. (*He pauses a moment, then adds one to the other. He watches, and then his eyes brighten*) It works—by God, it really works. It does react! (*Looking closely at the dish*) Mr Foulton, I salute you, charlatan though you be. (*With mounting excitement, he writes*) "Reaction positive. Repeat." No—no. No need to repeat. The mixture has a clear sympathy with the cerebelite of the brain. What is chemical must be controlled by chemicals. Physic unto physic. Something tells me this is going . . . Dreams, Dr Jekyll? Dreams have been the death of many. Hopes, Dr Jekyll, they have been the salvation of more. (*Calming down, he reads*) "Confirm . . . Two: add Foulton's Mixture to own compound." (*He takes a carefully wrapped bottle from the carrying box, unwraps and opens it*) Add one drop of Foulton's Mixture to own compound. (*He pauses, takes a noticeable breath, then adds a drop of the mixture to the bottle. He looks at the bottle, his eyes shining*) Three: test. Three . . . test. (*He pours a dose from the bottle into a small glass*) Test. (*His hand shakes as he holds the glass*) Mustn't get carried away. (*He puts the glass down*) All things in order. (*Writing*) "Standard dose plus one drop of F.M. Time— nine fifteen. Condition normal." (*He starts tidying his apparatus*) Condition normal. How can condition be normal when one may well be as near to God as conscious man will ever be? Or as near to the Devil? Blast Utterson. Now, the notes are written—the apparatus cleared. And the house is quiet. (*He picks up the glass*) Who is this fellow you try it out on? Hah. There is little he can do in this world . . . What did I call him? Hyde, that was it! Edward Hyde. Wonder why I picked that name. "Seems quite pleased to be able to help." (*He writes*) "Feel confident about this—" Damn it, I always feel confident. "Will retroversion—" Enough. (*Laying down his pen, he takes up the glass*) There is only one way to find out. Number three— test! Edward Hyde, I salute you. (*He pauses and then drinks the dose deliberately. He waits for a few moments, then takes up his pen and disappointedly begins to write*) No. "No reaction." (*He stares in front of him. His face gradually changes expression as the drug takes effect*) My God. My dear God. (*His face shows the pain he is suffering. The pain becomes intolerable*) What's happened? It's never been like this before. Ha ha. Must write it down. (*He manages to open his notes but the pen flies from his grasp*) Where am I? Why can't I see? Leave me alone! Must write. Pen. (*He tries to control himself*) I am Dr Henry Jekyll. Dr Henry Jekyll, M.D., D.C.L., F.R.! No—NO! I am Henry . . . Leave me alone.

The door opens and Charlotte enters tentatively

Leave me alone, I say! (*He backs away from the light*) I can't stand it. I can't—I can't . . . (*Sobbing, he slumps in the corner behind the armchair. He completes the transformation into Hyde as Charlotte speaks—see Production Notes*)

Charlotte What's wrong, sir? Can I help, sir? Oh dear. (*She peers into the* *gloomy corner)* I'll get Mr Poole. He'll kill me. (*She stands, scared and not knowing what to do*)

Jekyll (as Hyde) makes low moans

I only wanted to say thank you, sir. I sat on the stairs to wait for you—to say thank you. Sir?

Hyde stops moaning. As Charlotte moves towards him, he emits a rasping growl, turns and moves into the light by the table, roaring. Charlotte screams and falls in a faint, as—

the CURTAIN *falls*

Scene 2

The same. Morning, three days later

Hilda, the parlour maid, and Charlotte are cleaning the room. Hilda polishes the table while Charlotte sets the fire. Charlotte lifts the bucket as though to apply the coal in one sweeping action

Hilda Not like that. Do you want us to have to dust the whole room again? Use the glove, do, and put the lumps on one at a time. And do hurry, we have been long enough over it already. (*She returns to her work*)

Charlotte picks up the large coal glove

Charlotte (*giggling*) I've never seen such a big glove. Both my hands go into it easy. Hello Mr Glove. (*She treats the glove as a puppet*) Hello Miss Charlotte. (*She laughs*) Sorry. (*She returns to her work*)

Hilda I wonder why I used to get through my work quicker before I had you to help?

Charlotte Sorry. Finished. What do I do now?

Hilda (*without looking up*) Put the glove and the bucket outside ready to go down.

Charlotte puts the glove and bucket outside the parlour door

Then dust the grate. And do hurry.

Charlotte (*dusting the grate*) I am hurrying.

Hilda Doctor's been in such a queer mood lately I don't want to still be here when he comes back.

Charlotte Did you hear him go on at Cook this morning? Just because his breakfast wasn't ready, and it was only half-past six. Fire wasn't even lit. What do I do now?

Hilda Better do the mantel again.

Charlotte (*dusting the mantel*) I mean, breakfast is never before eight. We hadn't even had ours.

Hilda I know, I was there.

Charlotte Then he didn't eat it when you brought it up. I thought Cook would have a turn. Is that all right?

Hilda Except for the candlestick.
Charlotte Oh. (*She puts it right*) I can't get over me being brought upstairs
like this.
Hilda Neither can I.
Charlotte Did I tell you what happened when Miss Celestine was here?
Hilda You did. Twice. Just the rug then we go.(*She polishes very deliberately*)

Charlotte takes up the brush and dustpan

Charlotte (*after a pause*) Hilda. Are you worried that Doctor is not satisfied
with your work or something?
Hilda Never had need of two parlour maids before.
Charlotte Don't be daft. You are the proper parlour maid—he just wants me
to know what to do in case you are ill again.
Hilda Ummm. Maybe—maybe not.
Charlotte What do you mean?
Hilda I don't know. (*She stops work for the first time*) How long have you
been with this house?
Charlotte Over six weeks now.
Hilda I've been here over six years, and Doctor has always been a good gentleman. Always polite, you knew where you were with him. But these last
few weeks he's different. This morning, I saw him, before all that business
over breakfast. I came in here on my way down as I always do, to draw
back the blinds—and he was in there. (*She points to the laboratory*)
Charlotte Before six?
Hilda I think he had been in there all night. Then he came out, took something
out of that desk and went back in and he didn't even see I was here. His
collar was undone, there was ink on his fingers and he had such a scowl
on his face. Not like the doctor at all.
Charlotte Perhaps he's ill.

There is the clatter of the bucket being knocked over, off L

*Jekyll limps in wearing an overcoat and holding his shin. Despite this, he is
in the best of humours*

*Charlotte falls to the rug and brushes it feverishly. Hilda stands back and bobs
a respectful curtsy*

Jekyll 'Pon my soul.
Hilda Oh sir, I'm sorry, sir.
Jekyll Who left that thing out there?

*Hilda instinctively looks towards Charlotte who brushes the carpet even more
vigorously*

I might have guessed.
Hilda We've just finished, sir. We'll be going directly, sir.
Jekyll No matter, I have business to attend to in here. (*He goes towards the
laboratory, turns at the door and looks at Charlotte*) Do stop before you get
through to the floor boarding, won't you?
Charlotte (*innocently*) Oh yes, sir.

Jekyll smiles, unlocks the door and goes into the laboratory. Hilda looks after him in amazement. Charlotte resumes brushing, less vigorously

What did he mean? Of course I'll stop before I get through to the floor boarding.

Hilda Well, I don't know. Never seen the like.

Charlotte Does he think I'm silly?

Hilda And after he had tripped over your bucket. (*To Charlotte*) He was making a joke.

Charlotte The doctor?

Hilda He was teasing you.

Charlotte (*giggling*) Well I never. Fancy, a gentleman like the doctor. "Do stop before you reach the floor boarding." Wait 'til I tell the others.

Hilda laughs as she collects the brooms

I can't get over it, never in my whole life have I had . . . specially not a gentleman like that. "Do stop before you . . . "

Hilda "Do stop before you go right through the floor."

They laugh together. There is the sound of the bucket being knocked over again, off. Charlotte and Hilda stop laughing and gather the rest of the cleaning materials

Poole enters, carrying the coal bucket. He also carries a key and a small tin

Poole (*looking straight at Charlotte*) You?

Hilda I told her—

Charlotte She told me not to leave it in the way—but I must have done—Mr Poole, sir.

Poole Downstairs.

Charlotte moves towards the parlour door, keeping out of Poole's range. Poole turns to Hilda, as Jekyll comes in from the laboratory

Oh, there you are, sir. Are you going out, sir?

Jekyll No I'm not, Poole—I've just come in.

He takes off his overcoat and deposits it in Charlotte's arms, to her amazement

Put that in the closet in the hall, there's a good girl.

Charlotte exits with the coat, as if in a trance

Poole and Hilda stand wide-eyed in astonishment. Jekyll goes to the bureau and takes out his notes. As he moves towards the laboratory, he gives the bucket a quizzical look

Was there something you wished to say, Poole?

Poole thrusts the bucket into Hilda's arms, trying to regain his dignity. Hilda tries to suppress her laughter

Poole Yes, sir. The boy from the locksmith has just called with this, sir, with instructions to wait until it had been tried; but as I had . . .

Jekyll Jove, that was quick. (*He takes the key from Poole*)

Poole But as I had no idea to which door it referred . . .

Jekyll No, you wouldn't. I took it in myself earlier this morning. (*He disappears into the laboratory*)

Poole (*to Hilda*) Get out. And get on with some work.

Hilda exits with all the cleaning materials, only just controlling her mirth. She shuts the door with her foot. There is a clatter, off, as something drops

Jekyll comes in from the laboratory

Jekyll It fits perfectly. Whatever Monk asks give him double.

Poole Yes, sir. He also returned the pattern, sir.

Jekyll (*taking the tin*) And give the boy a penny for himself for being so quick.

Poole Very good, sir. About luncheon, sir.

Jekyll I leave it to Cook. Any time she likes.

Poole I mean, will you be taking any luncheon today, sir?

Jekyll Of course I will. Don't bother me now, I have work to do.

Poole As you say, sir.

Poole exits

Jekyll Luncheon, who knows where I shall be for luncheon. (*After a pause*) Yes. We are just about ready. Get my notes right up to date and then . . .

There is a tap at the door

Dr Jekyll is not at home this morning. (*He quickly goes into the laboratory, closing the door behind him. He busies himself at the workbench*)

Hilda enters from the hall, followed by Lanyon

Hilda Dr Lanyon, sir. Oh, I'm sorry, sir; I thought the doctor was here. If you will take a seat I'll see if I can find him for you.

Poole enters

Poole That will do, Hilda.

Hilda Do you know where I might find the doctor, Mr Poole?

Poole That will do, Hilda. Go downstairs and tell Charlotte to wash her hands and then come up here.

Hilda Charlotte, sir?

Poole Charlotte! She'll be wanted.

Hilda Very good, Mr Poole.

Hilda bobs a curtsy to Lanyon and exits

Lanyon I received a note.

Poole I trust you will forgive the liberty—but I sent it.

Lanyon Did you! Don't know what is happening to the world. Dr Jekyll shall hear of this. Where is he?

Poole With respect, sir. I am most concerned about the master and could think of no-one better to consult than his most respected friend.

Lanyon Servants sending notes, whatever next. You are not sickening for something are you Poole, and going off your head?

Poole I assure you, sir, that my unusual action was prompted only by my concern for the master's well being.

Lanyon Well, seeing that you have got me here and it is your master's health that worries you you'd better enlighten me. It's just as well for you that I am one of the more progressive in my attitude to the menial classes, that is all I can say.

Poole Yes, sir. Thank you, sir.

Lanyon Get on with it then. And I hope for your sake it is something important.

Poole Yes, sir.

Lanyon A glass if you please. Help me think. (*He sits*) I suppose Henry— Dr Jekyll—is not in there. (*He points to the laboratory*) Should hate to have him know I was listening to servants behind his back.

Poole (*pouring a glass of wine and giving it to Lanyon*) I cannot say for certain where the doctor is; but that door is particularly thick and transmits no sound whatsoever.

Lanyon (*looking at the laboratory*) Strange place. Henry did tell me what it was built for. Used to belong to a surgeon—that's it—used those old rooms as a dissection room. Um. Well get on with it, Poole; it's a pleasant day and I would care for a walk before luncheon.

Poole These last few days, sir, the master's behaviour has been more than usually unpredictable.

Lanyon He is inclined to be unconventional, you know what he is like.

Poole That's just it, sir. I do know what he is like; and there is something in his actions of late that give me a deep feeling of unease. In all my years of service for him . . . He has not been to his bed for two nights. Comes in and out without any warning at the most unlikely hours. Does not eat.

Lanyon He is just busy with his research.

Poole Riles at the staff one minute and jokes with them the next. Goes to the tradesmen unshaven.

Lanyon (*impressed by these last two points*) Not like him. Not like him at all.

Poole Then there is that girl.

Lanyon Girl? What girl?

Poole That little Graycape.

Lanyon She still here?

Poole She is, sir. Instead of dismissing her as was his clear duty he allows her to continue to work upstairs and sometimes treats her with a familiarity that I find quite incredible.

Lanyon Don't presume to correct your betters, Poole.

Poole I mean no such thing. I am just concerned for the master's well being.

Lanyon Very well, I'll have a word with him. I'll soon twig whether there is anything the matter.

Poole hesitates

Well?

Poole There is the incident of the other night, sir. After you and Miss Celestine had left, Mr Utterson stayed but a short time longer.

There is a tap at the door

(*Calling*) Wait! The doctor ordered the house to retire very early and gave strict instructions that he was not to be disturbed. Some while after, I am not certain how long, I thought I heard voices from this floor. I could only assume that the doctor had roused one of the servants for some reason. And then suddenly quite clearly I heard a woman scream.

Lanyon What did you do about it?

Poole There was little I could do. The doctor had specifically stated that he was not to be disturbed. I stayed where I was.

Lanyon Quite right. The rest of the house?

Poole Asleep in the garret or the outhouses, they could have heard nothing.

Lanyon Is that it then?

Poole Except that—I remained on the landing for some minutes but heard nothing further; I was just returning to my room when I heard a tread on the stair. I'll not be certain as there was very little light but I'll swear that it was that wretched little Graycape that crept passed me and went on up to the garret.

Lanyon Ummm. (*To himself*) Treats her with familiarity—can't be. (*To Poole*) What have you done about it?

Poole I was uncertain—I did nothing.

Lanyon Yes, perhaps it's as well.

Poole She is waiting outside the door, I thought you might like to question her.

Lanyon Me? Don't like to interfere in another man's affairs. It's up to Dr Jekyll. (*He looks at Poole*) Yes . . . better have her in, I suppose.

Poole (*calling*) Come in.

Charlotte enters, followed by Hilda

Come here. Stand there. Dr Lanyon wants to ask you some questions. (*To Hilda*) Go back and get on with your work.

Charlotte gives a frightened look to Hilda

Hilda (*to Lanyon*) Can't I stay, sir? I think she would be able to answer better if I was here

Lanyon Perhaps you are right—good idea.

Charlotte Thanks, Hilda.

Poole Be quiet. And answer the doctor truthfully.

Charlottte I always do.

Lanyon Now look here—um . . .

Hilda Her name's Charlotte, sir.

Lanyon What happened last Monday night?

Charlotte Monday?

Lanyon After my niece and I had left—what happened?

Charlotte Monday? Nothing, sir—oh, you mean about the lamp, yes I got into trouble because of the lamp. Is that what you mean, sir?

Lanyon I do not. I mean after the house had retired to bed. What happened?

Charlotte After?—No, nothing, sir.

Lanyon (*forestalling Poole*) You said you would tell me the truth, you know.

Charlotte hesitates

Come along, girl.
Hilda She's afraid, sir.
Lanyon Of me?
Hilda No, of him. And her position.
Lanyon She has nothing to fear if she tells the truth, she has my word on that.
Poole She will have something to fear if she doesn't.

There is a pause

Hilda You had better tell them—whatever it is.
Charlotte I wanted to say thank you to Doctor, that's all, honest. I just wanted to say thank you. So I sat on the stairs and waited. I came back down when everybody had gone. (*To Poole*) I stepped over the third stair that creaks. I waited a long time—I could hear the doctor moving about in the parlour, but he didn't come out. I thought he was alone but then all of a sudden he starts calling out, saying "Go away—go away". I was frightened, I didn't know what to do. I was afraid for the doctor too. So I went down to see if I could help. (*To Lanyon*) Was that right?
Lanyon Carry on, just carry on.
Charlotte (*becoming more scared*) I went in—there was one lamp on the table—but it was dark. The doctor was in the corner calling for help. (*She pauses—then suddenly*) It wasn't him. I went to him but it wasn't him. It looked like him but it wasn't him. It was horrible. (*She goes to Hilda for comfort*)
Hilda What happened next, Charlotte?
Charlotte (*recovering*) Horrible eyes. I don't remember much else except that look; and those eyes—I must have passed out—I remember something getting knocked over in there (*she points to the laboratory*) as I went back up stairs . . . My blouse got torn somehow—took me half the night to mend it.
Lanyon Incredible. Doesn't make sense.
Poole How dare you make up a pack of lies like that?
Charlotte I didn't make it up—I did see him. Believe me.

Utterson's voice is heard outside the parlour door

Utterson (*off*) All right, all right; I can see myself up. I know the way, should do by now.

Utterson enters

Where's Henry? Oh, hello Lanyon, have you been sent for too? I'm in a hurry, where's Henry? (*He moves towards the laboratory*) In here I suppose. Henry! (*He sees Poole and the maids*) Entertaining the servants. Lanyon? You in there . . .?

Jekyll comes in from the laboratory, carrying his notes

Jekyll Quite a room full. Good-day, Utterson, I have something for you. I had no idea you were calling too, Lanyon.

Poole goes to dismiss the maids

They can stay, Poole, I have instructions for all the staff.
Utterson I have an appointment with a crusty old judge in one half-hour.
Jekyll Then I will not delay you. (*He takes an envelope from his pocket*) As custodian of my legal affairs will you keep this in safety?
Utterson Of course. Is it something urgent?
Jekyll It could prove so—it is my will.
Utterson (*taking the envelope*) I would have gambled that would have lasted 'til later in the morning. Good-day.

Utterson exits

Jekyll Now Poole, I have some special instructions for the staff. (*To Lanyon*) You will excuse me?
Lanyon Of course—of course. I just thought I'd call as I passed and see how you were, that's all.
Jekyll I am in fine fettle—couldn't be better. (*To Poole*) Assemble the entire staff and tell them that from this day on, if at any time—any time whatsoever—a Mr Hyde calls or is encountered he is to have complete access to and freedom of the house; and is to be treated with due respect and courtesy. Is that clear?
Poole How will we recognize him, sir?
Jekyll Ah—I expect he will announce himself. He will be about my size.
Charlotte (*to Hilda*) That must be who I met the other night.
Jekyll You met the other night? What do you mean?
Charlotte Nothing, sir. I didn't mean anything.
Jekyll Funny child you are. That's all then, Poole.
Poole Yes, sir. Thank you, sir.

Poole, Hilda and Charlotte exit

Jekyll Now, my friend, what can I do for you? I am rather busy.
Lanyon Well—I just called—as I passed—see how you were. Must be going myself. I'd like to have another word with Poole if I may—about—the health of the servants—after the sickness, you know.
Jekyll By all means. By the way; come our meeting next Friday I think I may have something rather interesting to relate. See you then.
Lanyon Friday—of course Friday. Tomorrow that is. Look forward to it.

Lanyon exits, rather flustered

Jekyll stands lost in thought for a moment, then opens his notes

Jekyll (*reading*) "This is the day then. I am now prepared. The F.M. addition to my own compound has proved successful and a second dose completes retroversion. No noticeable after-effects." If only I could recall more than the general feeling—this time I shall remember. "That which I have sought for so long will this day be realized. Man is free from the cloak of man-made convention, man as he truly is. (*More quickly*) These notes are an accurate account of my work to date. Should any event prevent my concluding them I wish this book to be passed to my fellows at the Royal Society so that they may benefit from and continue the incredible studies of Henry Jekyll." That sounds a little pompous—never mind. (*He locks away his notes in the bureau drawer*) The next entry should be very interesting indeed. (*He turns suddenly*) Odd, why do I feel I am being overlooked? Strange doubts I sense. (*He looks at his watch*) A little after ten, within minutes I shall be—what I am. (*He moves to the laboratory and opens the door*) I shall open a door on truth. I shall step across the threshold—(*he goes through the doorway*)—to where only God and I shall know. (*He shuts the door behind him. During the next few speeches, he busies himself at the bench*)

After a pause, a disturbance is heard off L, then Utterson sweeps in, envelope in hand, Charlotte follows him

Utterson Henry! Where the devil are you, Henry?! Where's he got to?
Charlotte Don't know, sir.
Utterson Confound the man.
Charlotte I'll try and find him, shall I, sir.

Poole enters

Utterson Poole, where's the doctor—is he in or out?
Poole I'm afraid I have no idea, sir.
Utterson Well, you should have. It's your place to know. (*To Charlotte*) Pour me a glass of port, I'm in need of it.

As Utterson speaks, Poole dismisses Charlotte with a sign. Charlotte hesitates between the two orders

Hurry up, girl, what's the matter with you all today?

Charlotte goes to the drinks table and pours a drink

Jekyll exits R from the laboratory. There is a short pause and then the sound of a door slamming off R

Front door, perhaps that's him.
Poole That was not the front door, sir.
Charlotte (*looking at the laboratory*) Sounded more through there . . . (*She tails off, realizing she should not have spoken*)
Utterson Where is he, Poole, you must know whether he is in the house or not.
Poole Normally I would, sir, but of late . . .

As Charlotte hands Utterson his drink, she starts to say something, then checks herself

Utterson Out with it girl. If you have anything to say—say it.
Charlotte It's only that we left the two doctors together here—and he put me on to the front door brass straight away and nobody came in or went out.
Utterson Oh.
Charlotte I mean, they couldn't have could they? Otherwise I would have seen them.

Poole That will do. (*He dismisses Charlotte*)

Utterson If he is in the house where the devil is he? (*He bangs on the laboratory door*) Henry!

Charlotte moves towards the parlour door. As she reaches it, Lanyon enters. She bobs a curtsy to him, and exits

Ah, Lanyon got Henry with you?

Lanyon Indeed I have not. I was hoping he could spare a few minutes, I thought he was still here.

Utterson Well, he ain't. (*To Poole*) Don't just stand there, man, see if you can find him.

Poole I will instruct the staff to do so immediately, sir.

Poole exits

Lanyon He is not in there, I suppose.

Utterson If he is, he doesn't answer.

Lanyon I thought you were engaged for the morning.

Utterson I am. Deuce take the man. Lanyon, what do you know about this fellow Hyde?

Lanyon Only that this very morning Henry gave the staff instructions to let him have free run of the house.

Utterson Did he? He is to have more than free run it would seem. According to this he is to be Henry's first and only real beneficiary. Listen to this . . . (*He takes the will from the envelope*)

Lanyon I say—um—another man's will.

Utterson (*reading*) "Henry Jekyll M.D., D.C.L. et cetera, et cetera . . . all my possessions . . ." Ah, here we are, ". . . my friend and benefactor Edward Hyde: but in the case of my disappearance or unexplained absence for any period exceeding three calendar months, the said Edward Hyde shall assume my life and style without further delay and free from any burden or obligation." I've never heard anything like it. There are a few trifling sums to members of the household.

Lanyon Or his disappearance for three months—deuced odd. I mean . . .

Utterson There is another oddity. He is to have free run of the house, is he?

Lanyon So I heard Henry say.

Utterson And I heard Henry say that Edward Hyde was just some poor devil in some hospital or other who was paralysed and couldn't even walk.

Lanyon There is something very wrong here. Poole was quite right to call me in. I resented it at first you know but—

There is an urgent knock at the door, and then Charlotte enters

Charlotte Oh, sirs. Please come and help. Where's the doctor? It was horrible—I'm sure he has killed the poor little mite. I must find the doctor. She was just lying there howling. She'll die I'm sure if I don't find him. He just walked all over her. I saw it. I saw it. It was . . .

Utterson Silence!! Calmly now.

Charlotte I've never seen anything like it. She was just running up the street and he came round the corner and knocked her right over.

Utterson Where, girl? Who?!
Charlotte A little girl. On the corner where the alley leads to the mews at the back here. This man walked all over her. I can't believe it. Must find the doctor.

Hilda enters

Hilda Is he here? Oh sorry, sirs.
Lanyon I will come. I am after all also a doctor . . .
Hilda Would you, sir. They are just bringing her in downstairs. (*She holds the door open*)

Lanyon exits, followed by Hilda

Charlotte I saw it all. I was just getting back to the brass, I saw her run by, funny little thing she was, I watched her as she ran up the road—then as she got to the corner—he came out of the alleyway. She went flying—then he just . . .
Utterson Who was it? Have you ever seen him before?
Charlotte No! No, 'course I haven't.
Utterson Which way did he go?
Charlotte He came up towards the house. But I didn't see—I came in to get help.

Utterson exits

I didn't know what to do. He was like a devil . . . (*She flops into a chair, and buries her face in her hands, taking deep breaths*)

Hyde backs in through the parlour door

Charlotte slowly raises her head and gasps as she sees him. Hyde turns round quickly. Charlotte rises and steps back

Hyde Well, well, well. If it ain't the pretty little one. (*He grabs her by the front of her blouse*) We've met before, ain't we?

Charlotte cannot answer

Lost our tongue, have we? You don't want to be afraid of me, no fun in being afraid. Where was it we met? Remind me.
Charlotte (*hypnotized by his eyes*) In here, sir.
Hyde (*letting her go*) In here—in this very room—at night. That's it, I've been here before—once. Ain't I? (*Suddenly threatening*) What do you know about me? (*Grabbing her again*) I said what do you know about me?
Charlotte Nothing, Mr Hyde, sir.
Hyde (*releasing her again*) Mr Hyde. That's it, I'm Mr Hyde, ain't I? Mr Edward Hyde. A gentleman of great importance in this house.
Charlotte Yes, sir. We had our orders this morning, sir.
Hyde Remind me. (*He lounges in the armchair*)
Charlotte You are to come and go as you please, sir.
Hyde Nice—very nice.
Charlotte An' we are to do what you say.

Hyde Ah, you are to do what I say, are you. That's nice too, very nice. Come here, let's have a proper look at you.

Charlotte slowly moves towards him

Yes, I might have some very interesting orders for you little 'un. One day— or one night.

Charlotte I don't know what you mean, sir.

Hyde No? Never mind—you'll soon find out. (*Leaning over her*) We'll find out together, eh? (*He laughs, then stops suddenly. With swift animal cunning*) One word from you that you have seen me and you won't live to find out anything. (*He goes swiftly to the laboratory door, turns and lecherously surveys her*) Nice. (*He goes into the laboratory, closing the door behind him*)

Charlotte can do nothing but stare at the laboratory door

Hyde moves into the part of the laboratory unseen by the audience and exits

Hilda and Lanyon enter through the parlour door, followed by Poole, who carries the injured child

Hilda I don't think she is breathing.

Lanyon In this for now.

Hilda and Lanyon pull forward the armchair and Poole places the Child in it

A rug for her, and some water, quickly.

Hilda exits as Utterson enters

Utterson No sign of the scoundrel. Seems to have just vanished.

Jekyll, now without his Hyde make-up, quietly slips into the laboratory

In the parlour, all attention is on the child. Jekyll suddenly opens the laboratory door. Charlotte swings round in fear

Jekyll (*standing in the doorway*) What's happened? (*He moves across the room to the child and is horrified by what he sees*) God in heaven, what manner of fiend did this?

Hilda enters with a bowl of water and a cloth

Surely no man can be so inhuman . . . (*He tends to the child*)

The Lights fade to a Black-out, as—

the CURTAIN *falls*

SCENE 3

The same. Six weeks later. Early afternoon

When the CURTAIN rises, Jekyll and Celestine are sitting at the table having lunch. They have just finished the main course. Poole, Hilda and Charlotte stand in attendance

Charlotte moves to the table and clears the plates on to a tray. Her gauche enthusiasm is still apparent but she is much more competent in her work. Hilda serves dessert. Poole brings a decanter of wine to the table

Celestine More. I vow I shall not be able to eat again for at least a week. (*To Poole*) No, no more wine. It is most unwise to take too much wine too early in the day. You agree, of course, Henry.

Poole starts to fill Jekyll's glass

Jekyll Yes. (*He stops Poole from filling his glass completely*) Yes, of course, dear.

Celestine surveys her dessert

Poole It's syllabub, ma'am. A mixing of brandy and cream.
Jekyll I hope you care for it, dear, it is often served—it is one of Cook's favourites.
Celestine (*tasting*) It is not at all unpleasant. Brandy and cream, you say. I must remember that. When it is my responsibility to arrange your meals with Cook I will get her to prepare it. During the winter I think—for dinner; and a little less sweet.

They eat. Hilda holds the door for Charlotte

Hilda (*aside to Charlotte*) I hope I'm in the kitchen when she is telling Cook.
Charlotte I hope I'm there when Cook is answering back.

Suppressing giggles, Charlotte exits with the tray

Hilda and Poole dutifully become part of the background

Celestine As I was saying. My uncle has read through the marriage deed that Mr Utterson has drawn up. He finds it quite acceptable and as he is my only really close relation I do not feel obliged to concern any other member of the family.
Jekyll Good—good.
Celestine There are several minor points to settle of course. There is the running of the house. I will have a completely free hand in that?
Jekyll Naturally, my dear. When I asked you to become my wife I anticipated that I would be relieved of household worries.
Celestine (*kindly*) That is not all, surely—there was some personal regard was there not, Henry?
Jekyll Truly there was. I have a great fondness for you, Celestine.
Celestine And I you.

Charlotte enters and quietly stands with Poole and Hilda

I see no reason why our marriage should not prove most agreeable to us both.

Jekyll silently toasts this statement

When I first received your letter suggesting that I return to London I could hardly believe it. Having spent so much of my life in so remote an area—

then to be faced with a future with the responsibility of a house in London, no less. I felt here was a chance to prove myself. (*She finishes her syllabub*)

Hilda begins to clear the table. Charlotte sweeps the crumbs. Celestine watches her coldly

(*With grudging praise*) Remarkable. Perhaps I shall be able to keep her after all; below stairs.
Jekyll We'll discuss it later.
Celestine No need to concern yourself, Henry. I shall manage the household for you.
Jekyll That will do, Poole. They can clear up later.

Hilda and Charlotte exit with the tray

Oh, Poole. I meant to ask you before, was everything as it should be in here first thing this morning?
Poole As far as I know, sir. What had you in mind?
Jekyll Only that I came in particularly late and—I must have been more than usually tired—I do not remember locking the laboratory door.
Poole Everything was just as it always is, sir.
Jekyll Force of habit, must have locked it without realizing. That's good. Thank you, Poole.
Poole Sir. (*He moves towards the parlour door*)
Celestine Poole.

Poole turns at the door

I fancy some tea. Tell Cook to prepare a pot and have it sent up.
Poole Yes, madam. For you, sir?
Jekyll Yes—I suppose so.
Poole As you say, sir.

Poole exits

Celestine A lovely meal, Henry. I really quite enjoyed it. Though I must confess that I am not at all used to eating at so early an hour.
Jekyll Bless me. I should have arranged it for this evening, shouldn't I? If I had a modicum of the romantic in me I would have known that it should have been candlelight for our little chat. (*Rising, he indicates the armchair*)

Celestine rises from the table and settles herself in the armchair. Jekyll remains standing

Celestine I feel our discussions were rather more important than "chat", dear. However I am very pleased that we have reached such amicable agreement— and, well, I do know that I am not marrying one of the most romantic gallants of the town.
Jekyll What sort of man are you marrying? (*He begins to move about the room*)
Celestine I flatter myself I have a good judgement of character. I think I understand the nature of the man who is to become my husband.
Jekyll Humm. I wish I did. A glass of wine? Oh no, we are having tea, aren't

we? As a matter of fact I have become quite used to a full luncheon, I seldom find myself in of an evening.

Celestine That reminds me. Another point that I would rather like to consider. My uncle tells me how of late you are hardly ever at home. More and more you seem to be out and about. To tell the truth, he is more than a little disappointed that you have not even found time for those little Friday evening get-togethers. Five weeks he says it is now.

Jekyll That is quite true. I have been particularly active these last few weeks; and I have found it wonderful.

Celestine I must admit that you do seem more—well, more alive.

Jekyll That's it exactly, Celestine. Alive—alive alive.

Celestine How strange you are sometimes. Uncle asked me to ask you—what was it now? An experiment, that's it, how is your experiment proceeding?

Jekyll Tell him it is concluded; it is a success but I don't know what the answer is—because I can never remember. Though sometimes I feel I nearly do. I feel the elation but not the facts.

Celestine Henry?

Jekyll Tell him he shall have a full report—one day.

Celestine Are you not well, Henry?

Jekyll Not well? I have never been better. My life is full, my existence has purpose. Few men can say as much.

Celestine And you are about to be married.

Jekyll Yes that too—the coin and its worth. (*He stops, wondering what made him say a thing like that*)

Celestine (*after a slight pause*) We were saying. Of late you have been spending much of your time with the lower orders I understand; tending their needs.

Jekyll Their needs—their fear—their despair.

Celestine I am not blaming you—I think it is most creditable of you. Do you actually go into their houses?

Jekyll Houses? Yes I go into their—houses.

Celestine What I mean is—I think I should know—after we are married, do you intend to continue with this work?

Jekyll Of course.

Celestine And with this—study of—the nature of man that you were so keen on?

Jekyll (*with a flash of Hyde in his look*) Of course!

Celestine But why, Henry? You used not to find it necessary to do so much.

Jekyll Why? Because I must. These people are ill, I am a doctor of medicine, I can help them. They are deprived, I am a doctor of law. I can advise them. I must do what I can. The evil in this world must be paid for and I am in a position to help pay.

Celestine I do not see why—you do not cause the evil.

Jekyll reacts to this, unseen by Celestine. His face shows a touch of Hyde

Jekyll (*controlling himself*) Celestine. I will undertake to abide by all of our marriage arrangement, I will be to the best of all my power as Dr Jekyll a good husband to you. You will have full jurisdiction over the household, saving my work area. (*He points to the laboratory*) Your own property will remain entirely at your own disposal. Your life will be well ordered and comfortable. All this I promise. But I must be free to come and go as I wish—to help whoever I choose, and I must continue my researches.

Celestine Of course, Henry. If that is what you want. I have no intention of standing in the way of your studies. I only ask that after we are married you carry them out at day and not during the night.

Jekyll No! Impossible. I only really come alive at night! (*He calms down*) I mean I have always worked better later in the day. But I promise that I will do my utmost to arrange my researches to cause you as little inconvenience as possible.

Celestine Thank you, dear. And as for those "good works" that you do for the poor; I understand all about them you know.

Jekyll looks surprised and worried

You feel you *must* help people. You feel it is your debt to help them. You feel you must fill your time doing good. I know why.

Jekyll Go on.

Celestine It happened five weeks ago, didn't it? Five weeks ago you were a stuffy old bachelor who cared for nothing but gaining knowledge for its own sake and now you are a knight in shining armour who will answer any cry for help no matter how grubby the caller. Five weeks ago something happened to change you—didn't it?

Jekyll (*defensively*) Remind me.

Celestine What a tease you are sometimes. Five weeks ago you asked me to become your wife.

Jekyll (*laughing with relief*) And a knight in shining armour is far more worthy of you than a stuffy old bachelor. How right you are.

Celestine I said I understood you.

There is a knock on the door and Poole enters, followed by Hilda with a tea tray and Charlotte, who carries an empty tray

Jekyll Ah, tea.

Poole Shall I take the opportunity and have the table cleared, sir?

Jekyll By all means.

Poole dispenses the tea while Hilda and Charlotte clear the table and remove the white tablecloth

Poole Will you take milk or sugar with your tea, madam?

Celestine Neither, thank you.

Poole The small son of the knife-grinder called, sir. He returned a phial of liquid that he says you left . . .

Jekyll What a fool the man is. I left it with him and told his wife to apply it to the wound every day. Sometimes people are very hard to help. Anything else to report, Poole?

Hilda and Charlotte exit with the tray and tablecloth

Poole Only that talk has it that Mr Hyde was in trouble again, sir. A fight at the *Black Boar* it seems.

Jekyll (*quickly*) When was this?
Poole Last night, sir, or very early this morning. A woman hurt, so it is said. What should I do if he comes here, sir?
Jekyll (*sharply*) Nothing Poole, you know your orders. This woman, was she hurt badly?
Poole I couldn't say, sir.
Celestine Come here? Why on earth should such a man come here?
Poole Master has given orders that Mr Hyde . . .
Jekyll (*pacing about*) Mr Hyde is very important to me, you could never understand, he is part of my researches—I owe a great deal to Mr Hyde. After all, he has a right to live has he not?
Celestine We will discuss it later, Henry. If you are helping him then I cannot object if he should occasionally call at the back door if that is your wish; whoever he is—but later. Do sit down dear, it is most disconcerting the way you keep pacing.
Jekyll I am sorry, I seem to have grown unaccustomed to inactivity. (*He sits on an upright chair*)

Celestine gives him a condescending smile

There is a tap at the door and Hilda enters quickly

Hilda Mr Poole, sir. An urgent message for the master.
Jekyll What is it, Hilda?
Hilda (*quickly*) Man has just called from the coal-yard, sir. Something broke on one of the waggons and a whole lot of coal fell off, it's trapped one of the girls that work there. Will you come down and talk to him, sir? (*She slows down under Celestine's gaze*)
Jekyll Of course I will. We will both come. (*To Celestine*) It will give you opportunity to see the kitchen and to meet Cook and the staff. (*To Hilda*) Tell them we are on our way.
Poole (*to Hilda*) I'll go. You clear up in here.

Poole exits

Hilda stands to one side, as Jekyll unlocks the laboratory door. His edgy restlessness has gone, and he is now alive and eager to be about his mission

Celestine Do you mean that you are going *now* to attend to this?
Jekyll (*going into the laboratory*) Of course. (*He packs various bottles into a bag*)
Celestine Cannot you go later? Why now?
Jekyll Because it is now that the help is needed.
Celestine But we still have matters to discuss.

Jekyll comes back into the parlour with his bag. He locks the laboratory door behind him, but in his haste, leaves the key in the lock

Jekyll We have the rest of our lives together for discussion, my dear. At this moment my skill and help are needed.
Celestine (*watching his urgency for a moment*) It is as if you were fighting something. As if your life depended on it.

Jekyll stops and looks at her seriously

Jekyll (*smiling*) Yes dear, I think it does. Come along now, I'll just have time to introduce you to Cook. (*He holds the door open*)

Celestine exits

(*As he goes*) It's wrong the way they still use these young girls as pickers, some of them are no more than seven or eight . . .

Jekyll exits

Hilda starts to collect the tea things together

Charlotte enters and helps her

Charlotte (*stopping*) Hilda. I think I'll leave.
Hilda Leave? Leave here? Why?—'cause of her?
Charlotte No—well yes, her too.
Hilda You can't. What will you do? Don't be daft, you are better off here— even if it is only in the scullery.
Charlotte (*resuming her work. To herself almost*) I'll run away—I'll find something—rag-picking, anything.
Hilda What's the matter? You are scared aren't you?

Charlotte doesn't answer or even look at her

Not of her? Poole?

Charlotte shakes her head

It can't be the master, he treats you as if . . . It isn't the master, is it?
Charlotte (*sharply*) No! It's the other one.

Hilda frowns, not understanding

That horrible Hyde bloke.
Hilda Lord-a-mercy girl! Stop worrying and get on.
Charlotte It's all right for you, you ain't seen him—I have. If you'd met him like I did you wouldn't . . .
Hilda But nobody has seen him for over a month now. We hear tales of what he has been up to but he hasn't actually been here since—since you saw him.
Charlotte (*quietly*) He was here last night. I'm sure. I woke up in the night. Don't know why but I went to the window; I couldn't see, the window is too high, but I heard someone cross the mews to the back of the house. It was him. I'd know that tread anywhere; the way he sort of drags one foot. He's come back, Hilda, and I don't know what to do.
Hilda (*kindly*) Let's get finished in here and we will talk about it downstairs.
Charlotte He got hold of me—and looked—he said he'd have some orders for me.
Hilda What sort of orders?
Charlotte Don't know. But he's been here again, I know it.

The door opens quietly and Celestine stands in the doorway

Hilda It was weeks ago. (*Suddenly noticing Celestine and changing her tone*) Come along Charlotte, pick up that linen. (*Looking at Celestine*) Oh, sorry, madam.

Hilda and Charlotte bob curtsys

Shall I leave the tea, madam?

Celestine No, take it.

The maids exit with the tea tray

How Henry managed with a household like this I cannot imagine. As for that Cook . . . (*She sees the key in the laboratory door and goes across to it. She stops, then takes the key out and puts it on the table*)

There is a knock at the door and Poole enters

Poole I am sorry to disturb you, madam, but there is a woman at the door. I told her that Doctor was out but she seemed to know that you were here.
Celestine What sort of woman? What does she want?
Poole Looked rather disreputable, madam. Mentioned Mr Hyde.
Celestine Send her away. No! Mr Hyde, the mysterious and evil Mr Hyde. I'll see her, Poole. She can answer a few questions for me. Send her up.
Poole In here, madam?
Celestine Do I not speak clearly?

Poole bows and exits

Poole (*off*) I thought I told you to wait in the hall.
Penny (*off*) Arh. Get twisted you old paste-horn.

The door opens and Penny stands defiantly in the doorway. She wears a shawl around her head. Poole glides in past her

Poole The—person, madam.
Celestine (*looking coldly at Penny*) Thank you, Poole.

Poole hesitates

Thank you, Poole. You may go!

Poole bows and exits

Penny (*returning Celestine's gaze*) You must be Jekyll's woman. I want to talk to you. (*She saunters into the room*)
Celestine (*with calm authority*) And I want to talk to you, you had better sit down. Over there. (*She indicates one of the upright chairs*)
Penny Huh, aren't we the high madam. (*She sits down*)
Celestine My name is Celestine Fitch-Grant. I am shortly to be married to Mr Henry Jekyll. You are sitting in what will soon be *my* withdrawing room; so please tell me the reason for your visit. (*She sits opposite Penny*) Your name is—?
Penny You're cool, I'll give you that. Cool—and cold. I pity him. Well since you ask, I was christened Penitence Gladworth; but I have known

no other name but Penny. And Edward Hyde is my bloke—and I am willing to fight for him. Even though I often curse him. Hell only knows who he is and where he came from but since he came around—he is for me!

Celestine I am sure you are admirably suited. But what has all this to do with me?

Penny This is what it has got to do with you. (*She lets fall the shawl that has been over her head and shows that one side of her face is badly grazed and bruised*) Last night there was a fight and he did that to me. Me!

Celestine (*turning away from the wounds*) Not unlike him from what I hear.

Penny But it is unlike him. 'Cause with me he is gentle. Gentle in such a way that you couldn't understand Missus High-blown Lady. 'Cause you've never had anyone touch you. But last night he was different, he wasn't himself at all; I thought he was ill, he kept saying "Go away Jekyll"—or something like that; then he took a little bottle out of his pocket and drank something. I thought he was going mad. He dragged me off down to the *Black Boar*, drank a bottle of gin nigh straight off and then near as a groat murdered some fellow for tripping over his leg. Would have done too if I hadn't got in the way. (*She gently feels her injured face*)

Celestine starts to interject

All right—all right. This is where you come in. When it looked as if the whole company was going to murder him he left. What he doesn't know is that I followed him. He didn't go back to his rooms—no not last night, he didn't go back there—he came here! I saw him let himself in round the mews. (*She stands and moves round to Celestine*) I love him—can you understand, I love him. I know he is no good, then neither am I; but no-one else ain't going to interfere between him and me; no-one! I ain't bleeding well going to let them. So you can tell your bloke to stop interfering—he can go round helping who he likes but you just tell him to leave my man alone. He's mine, he's all I've got. And in his way he loves me; gentle—hard—and real! Not that you'd know anything about that.

Celestine Why you working people assume that you are the only ones to know what love is I can never understand.

This approach surprises Penny

Yes. I too love a man. Not as you in an animal earthy way. But in a civilized educated manner we love each other. It's easy for your sort to go round doing what you like when you like; but those born with a position in life bear God's responsibility for those less favoured.

Penny I didn't come here for any sermon, missus.

Celestine If you must call me anything I would prefer "madam".

Penny I'll call you Celestine if you like.

Celestine Sit down and be quiet. (*She points to a chair*)

Penny sits, but not in the chair indicated

I wish to know more of how Dr Jekyll is connected with your—Edward Hyde.

Penny I ain't sure. Seems afraid of him sometimes. I know he can have free run of this place if he wants. Oh, he ain't been here lately. Not since your bloke rented these lodgings for him.

Celestine When was this?

Penny Umm. About five weeks ago. I'm not grumbling about them mind—they come in very handy, except that I only see him at night, and not always then.

Celestine (*pondering a moment*) You can be assured that Mr Hyde will not come into this house any more.

Penny You mean it's all right then? Eh, you ain't so bad after all. You might be real after all under all that casing.

Celestine Emotion is not the prerogative of the poor. But do not misunderstand me. I said that your Mr Hyde will not come here again; I did not say that I would prevent Dr Jekyll trying to help him. Quite the contrary, it is our duty to try and help those less well-placed—even if it is against their wishes.

Penny You bleeding old hypocrite. (*Rising*) You're all the stinking same. I was nearly thinking you were almost human. There ain't (*she snaps her fingers*) that much love in you at any level.

Jekyll enters, bag in hand. He does not immediately see Penny

Penny reacts to him, her face showing interest, doubt then fear

Celestine Hello dear, you haven't been long.

Jekyll (*putting his bag on the table*) No, the poor child was dead. She was no more than nine. Nine years of utter misery, she could never . . . (*He stops short as he comes face to face with Penny*)

Neither Penny nor Jekyll move as they look at each other

Celestine This person called to see you.

She continues talking as fear grows on the confronting faces of Jekyll and Penny

She seems to resent your trying to help people, has some rather strong views on the relations between men and women. Seemed to think that a basic connection gave one some kind of power of possession over the other. I told her we are what we are, good or bad, and that the good must always try to help the bad. (*She comes forward, joining Jekyll and Penny*) She was very strong in her views. (*To Penny*) Well, have you nothing to say to Dr Jekyll?

Penny stands as if trying to overcome some power from Jekyll. She breaks away

Penny No I ain't. I've said all I've got to say. (*She moves limply to the door, then turns to face Jekyll. Desperately*) Bleeding keep away from Edward Hyde.

Celestine Really!

Penny Go to hell!

Penny swings out, slamming the door behind her

Jekyll still stands unmoving. Hyde is gradually creeping into him

Celestine Disgusting creature.

Jekyll (*trying to collect his thoughts*) Nine—yes—nine years old. Poor mangled little body. (*Raising his voice*) It's evil. Something should be done about such evil!
Celestine Don't shout, dear.
Jekyll I'm sorry, perhaps a glass of wine. (*He goes to the sideboard, pours out a drink and gulps it down*)
Celestine You are not unwell are you, Henry?

He smiles and shakes his head

You spend far too much effort on these errands of mercy as you call them.
Jekyll But you know I must do all I can for these people.
Celestine I don't see why. Anyway you can hardly call them—"people".
Jekyll (*sitting and making a good if conscious show of normality*) Don't be so old-fashioned, dear. By the by, what did that poor girl want who was here just now?
Celestine She was concerned for the man she loves.
Jekyll (*smiling at her*) Isn't every woman?
Celestine She thinks you are trying to influence him. His name is Edward Hyde apparently.

Jekyll rises and turns away, burying his face in his hands

(*Not seeing this move*) I told her that Edward Hyde would not be allowed in this house again.
Jekyll (*recovering; defiantly*) Edward Hyde will not be allowed in this house again!
Celestine Yes Henry, that is what I said. I am glad you agree . . .

Jekyll is trying to maintain his own personality

Henry—who is this Edward Hyde? What is it about him?
Jekyll (*deliberately*) We must not talk about Hyde. Not now!
Celestine But I want to know, I insist.
Jekyll And I say no!
Celestine You have never spoken to me like that before. (*Looking hard at him*) What is the matter—something is wrong.

He avoids her gaze

It's not like you at all. I can always rely on your good manners. Did the sight of that poor little child upset you?

He still keeps his back to her

Henry—let me have a look at you. I am sure you are sickly.
Jekyll (*his voice not quite his own*) I am not. For God's sake stop talking.
Celestine Henry . . .
Jekyll And don't keep calling me Henry! (*Making a determined effort, he straightens up and goes to the laboratory door. More to himself*) Excuse me Celestine, I must . . . (*He sees the key is not in the lock and desperately fumbles in his pocket for it. Then, with tragic calm*) Do you know what has happened to the key to this door?

Celestine Yes—it's . . .

Jekyll (*shouting*) Where is it?

Celestine (*shaken*) I put it on the table—there it is.

Jekyll (*with controlled desperation*) Celestine—do as I say. Go down into the
hall and wait for me.

She hesitates

If you have any love for me at all do as I say!

Celestine exits

*Jekyll lets out a rasping sigh of relief and rushes to the table. His face now has
Hyde's expression. Grabbing at the key, he knocks it on to the floor. He bends
and picks it up. As he straightens up, his face shows the struggle going on within
him*

Must get into the laboratory . . . Must go and get . . . (*He does not move*)
No-no-no! (*He suddenly throws the key away, laughing Hyde's laugh. He looks
surprised and terrified*) No—it cannot . . . Nooooooo . . . (*He collapses behind
the table, moaning and sobbing. The actor should now complete the transformation into Hyde—see Production Notes*)

*The moaning sobs suddenly stop. After a slight pause, Hyde's face slowly appears
from behind the table. He looks round and smiles in triumph. He stands up slowly*

Hyde (*with a satisfied chuckle*) Mustn't keep me away. That wouldn't be nice
at all. Not nice at all.

The Lights fade to a Black-out as—

the CURTAIN *falls*

ACT II

The same. One month later. The events in this scene take place during the course of one week

Evening. There is a glimmer of light from the lamp on the table

> *Jekyll enters, wearing his overcoat and carrying his bag. He is tired to the point of exhaustion. He takes off his coat and puts it over a chair. He turns up the lamp, then goes to the bureau and brings his notes, pen and ink to the table. He sits down*

Jekyll (*writing*) "Thirty-three days now. Felt slightly more secure today. Hard work seems to keep him at bay." (*Making correction*) Musn't call it him. " . . . *it* at bay." Oh God. I'm so tired. It must end soon surely. (*He sits with his head in his hands*)

> *There is a slight tap at the door and Charlotte enters quietly with a tray of food. She stands at the table by Jekyll*

(*Starting*) Eh! Oh, it's you. Thank you, Hilda.
Charlotte Charlotte, sir.
Jekyll Um. Little Charlotte? So it is.
Charlotte (*putting the tray in front of him*) It's cold beef again, sir, and some ale. (*She draws the curtains and picks up his coat*)

Jekyll does not eat

You're later than ever tonight, sir. You must be ever so tired.
Jekyll I am, Charlotte. More tired than anyone can know.
Charlotte Is it all right, sir? I could try and find something different if you like, sir; before I go to bed.
Jekyll No, this will suffice. (*He still does not eat*) You had better cut along. It must have been a long day for you.
Charlotte It'll be a short night, I've got to be up again in a few hours. (*She goes to door and looks back at the motionless figure*) Good-night, sir.

Jekyll still gives no response. Charlotte goes back to him and stands, concerned but powerless

Jekyll (*without looking up*) Are you happy with life?
Charlotte I suppose so. Yes, sir. (*After a pause*) It's better here than at the House. It was bitter cold there in winter—but here, I've got a mattress of my own to sleep on—and sometimes some of the girls have a bit of fun.
Jekyll (*looking up and smiling*) What do your friends call you?
Charlotte Haven't really got any. Hilda and some of the others call me Lottie

sometimes. (*She starts to giggle to herself*) They call me Dotty Lottie. (*She laughs*) But Hester in the scullery, we call her Sniffy. (*She giggles self-consciously*) Do you know why, sir?

Jekyll (*smiling*) I can guess. (*He looks at her*) Lottie—little Lottie. Lottiekins. That's it; I shall call you Lottiekins. It suits you.

Charlotte (*with simple grateful pleasure*) Lottiekins—oh I like that; thank you, sir. Oh, but please, sir, not when Mr Poole is here. I don't want to get into trouble.

Jekyll (*more relaxed*) How right you are, we mustn't get into trouble from Mr Poole, must we? (*He looks at her then becomes very serious*) I want you to do something for me. (*He goes and unlocks the laboratory door*) This is very serious, could be the difference between life and death.

Charlotte Whose?

Jekyll (*profoundly*) I have no way of knowing. (*He goes into the laboratory*) I feel I can trust you. A great deal may depend upon you at any time. (*He returns with a small bottle of physic and locks the door*) Mr Hyde . . .

Charlotte jumps at the name

Mr Hyde has gone away. I hope he will never return. If he ever does I think he will look for you, do not be afraid, Lottiekins, this medicine will make him better and he will not hurt you. Tell him that Dr Jekyll says he *must* drink it. I'll put it here in my desk. (*He puts the bottle in the bureau*) You are free to go to it at any time. (*He pauses*) You have nothing to say? No questions?

Charlotte No, sir. I hope he never comes back, but if he does I'll try and do what you say.

Jekyll (*almost affectionately*) You must go to bed now. Good-night—Lottie-kins.

Charlotte (*with a giggle at the name*) Good-night, sir.

Charlotte exits with the coat

Jekyll looks after her for a moment, then returns to his notes

Jekyll What an untidy mess. (*He looks back through the pages*) It used to be neat enough. Is this round hand the same as this irregular scrawl? (*Writing*) "The child's innocence has made me think more clearly. Proposition. I did not release my own personality after all, but allowed my brain to create something new." (*Looking up and thinking ahead*) And being imaginary it is not bound by normal human limitations. I am a normal human being—that means that I cannot—like a runaway waggon on a steep hill, no matter how hard the waggoner pulls at the brake there is no stop 'til the crash at the bottom. (*Scared by the ultimate doom of this theory*) No, there must be another theory. Jekyll must be stronger than Hyde. Jekyll is real. I am real, I am stronger. I'll prove that I am stronger. But which I am I? It's no good, I can do no more tonight. I must have sleep. (*Wearily, he puts his notes, pens and ink away in the bureau and turns down the lamp*)

Jekyll exits

There is a Black-out to denote the passing of time. During the Black-out, Jekyll's bag and the tray from the table are removed, and the curtains are opened at the window

It is now morning on a dull day. The Lights come up on Lanyon and Celestine, who are sitting at the table, and Utterson, who sits in the armchair. They are waiting for Jekyll. There is a long pause

Lanyon Yesterday he was abed and could not be roused; today he is out and cannot be found. I'm disappointed in the fellow, Celestine.

Celestine (*with a simple honesty*) So am I, Uncle.

Lanyon Yes. Well. (*Rising*) You staying on, Utterson?

Utterson I am used to waiting.

Lanyon Come along, my dear, we will try again tomorrow. Fellow must be in some time.

Celestine rises disappointedly

(*With well-intended but tactless jocularity*) I mean, if you are going to marry the chap you must meet him some time, mustn't you?

Celestine One would have thought so.

Lanyon We will tell Poole—ah, here he is.

Poole enters, followed by Charlotte carrying a tray of food, and Hilda, who holds a tablecloth in one hand. Her other arm is obviously causing her a lot of pain

Poole Dr Jekyll has just returned, sir. Would you excuse me, he insists on dining without delay.

Hilda and Charlotte prepare the table, moving the lamp on to the sideboard and spreading the tablecloth

Celestine Did you tell Henry that we had called as arranged and that we were still waiting?

Poole I did, madam.

Charlotte exits

Hilda sets out the dishes with one hand

(*Sensing her next question*) He went upstairs, madam, to clean up, he was somewhat dirty from the fire. (*He bows and goes to leave*)

Celestine (*coldly*) What fire?

Poole Just before dawn, madam, it seems a store of jute took fire at Shadwell Wharf. The master saw the glow and went to see if he could help.

Utterson And did he?

Poole I gather there are several people who will live to be grateful for his efforts, sir. (*To Celestine*) If you will excuse me, I will see if he requires my services.

Poole bows and exits

Utterson It's almost as if he wants to kill himself—I wonder why?

Celestine (*sitting*) I am certain that something has happened to Henry in some way, but we will never learn what it is from that man.

Hilda drops a piece of cutlery. The others look at her

Hilda Sorry, sir. Sorry, madam. (*She continues laying the table*)
Lanyon What's the matter with your arm, girl?
Hilda It got knocked, sir. It will be all right.
Utterson Come here.

Hilda goes to him reluctantly

Who knocked it?
Celestine I suppose it was Poole.
Hilda (*quickly*) No, madam.
Lanyon A footman?

Hilda does not answer

Utterson That only leaves Dr Jekyll.

Hilda's expression shows he is right

(*Stilling the others*) Tell us.

No answer

(*Sharply*) When?
Hilda It was this morning, sir. I came in to draw the blinds. First down always draws the blinds, Doctor insists. Well he used to—doesn't seem to mind much about anything now. Well, when I came in it was dark but I heard a sort of breathing sound and I realized that he was asleep in that chair, sir. The one you are sitting in.
Utterson You are sure it was the doctor?
Hilda Who else, sir?
Utterson What did he say?
Hilda I suppose I must have disturbed him when I came in, 'cause I didn't expect him to be here. But then he didn't exactly say anything he just— well—growled, sir.
Celestine Really!
Utterson And then he hit you?
Hilda Well—no, sir.
Celestine Either you were hit or you were not, which was it?
Hilda It was when I went to draw the blinds, madam. He seemed to wake up suddenly. He lurched across the room and hit my arm away. Ooo, it did hurt. And he kept saying "No—no" all funny. Then he went off into there. (*She points to the laboratory*) I don't think he was properly awake though because his voice sounded different and he seem to walk funny.

There is a pause

Utterson Continue.
Hilda Nothing else, sir. I think he must have a drink of some sort in there because I heard the sound, he must have dropped the glass—it broke. Then

he came out and said he must go and see if he could help. At the fire—
yes, he said at the fire.

Utterson Saw the glow through the back window I suppose. How did he seem
then?

Hilda Oh, wide awake, sir. Quite himself.

Utterson And all he said was "No"—twice? I must know.

Hilda (*trying to remember*) "No—no." Oh, as he went out he said something
like—"Not again—not after all this time." Or something like that. But he
was only muttering.

Lanyon She's making it all up.

Hilda does not answer, but stares at him unwaveringly

Utterson I want you to think very carefully. Is it possible that there is someone
else in the house? Hiding—say in there? (*He points to the laboratory*)

Lanyon Utterson, you don't think that . . .

Utterson stills him

Hilda (*thinking a moment*) No, sir, it's too quiet. And if there is he doesn't
eat anything.

Utterson dismisses her, and she returns to the table

Lanyon You are not suggesting surely that . . .

Utterson I am not suggesting anything, Lanyon, because I just don't know
what to suggest. But the fellow ain't himself and I want to know why.

Celestine And so do I.

The door opens and Poole admits Jekyll

Poole The master.

Jekyll (*very much his old self*) My dear Celestine. (*He kisses her hand*) Lanyon,
I do apologize, but no doubt you heard that my services were required.
Utterson, I didn't expect to see you here.

Utterson One does not know what to expect these days it seems.

Their defensiveness is being deflated by Jekyll's naturalness

Jekyll (*sitting at the table*) Will you excuse me if I dine? I am ravenous, I
haven't eaten since—I really cannot remember when.

Hilda serves Jekyll at the table. He suddenly notices her damaged arm

Celestine Henry. Things cannot go on as they are, somewhen we must meet
and reconsider our arrangement.

Jekyll Of course, my dear—any time. (*To Hilda*) Your arm, how did you hurt
it?

Hilda does not answer but rather draws back

Let me see.

She lifts her arm. He rolls back the sleeve and examines it very gently

My soul, this was a wicked knock. I wonder the bone is not broken. (*His
manner changes as he recalls Hyde. He drops the arm*)

Hilda hastily exits

The others watch not understanding

(*Fighting to keep his normality*) You were saying, my dear, about our arrangement.
Celestine If arrangement there be. (*Rising*) I will call on you tomorrow at ten. (*She goes to the door, holding back tears*) When I trust you will be more yourself.

Celestine exits. Lanyon follows dutifully

Jekyll (*sincerely*) Pray God I am. And you, Utterson?
Utterson Do you want me to leave?
Jekyll As I value your friendship—and if you value mine—it may be wiser if you did.

Utterson rises and looks at him, as though offering help

No, my friend. (*Tense and strained*) No-one can help.
Utterson I'll bid you good-day then Jekyll; and leave you to your own devices.

Utterson exits

Jekyll My own devices—ha!

The Lights fade to a Black-out. During the Black-out, the dishes, tray and white tablecloth are cleared from the table; the lamp and Jekyll's notebook, pen and ink are set on the table

Evening. The Lights come up on Jekyll sitting at the table without his jacket. His head is in his hands, he could be asleep. After a pause, he looks up, a tired, gaunt, desperate figure

Jekyll (*with great effort*) Whatever happens I must keep the record. Let's see, what have I put? (*He reads*) "Twenty-fourth. The elation of the first weeks is now equalled by despair. I long, how I long for the freedom and delight that the physic offers." God, how true. I musn't. "I still cannot bring myself to give up the rooms in Soho. I am scared of what it is in me that prevents the rest of me taking this obvious step. Hyde still has a grip on Jekyll even when he is Jekyll. Concentration more difficult—sleep more frightening." Dreams and reality are too mixed. (*Making a correction*) "Sleep is im—poss—ible!" (*He writes so violently that he breaks the pen. His movements are becoming random. He gets up, goes to the bureau and rummages around for another pen. He knocks the bottle of physic on to the floor, picks it up and tosses it back, then stops. He retrieves the bottle and brings it to the table. He puts it in the light of the lamp, sits down and looks at it. Desperately*) No! (*He rises and sweeps to the door, flinging it open*)

Charlotte can be seen in the hallway, duster in hand. They look at each other, and then Jekyll comes back into the room. Charlotte follows him

Charlotte Did you want something, sir?
Jekyll Did I want something! Hah!! (*He suddenly becomes less tense*) No. No I don't want anything.

Charlotte Shall I do the blinds while I am here, sir?

Jekyll mumbles assent, and stands unmoving as Charlotte draws the curtains. As she goes back towards the door, she notices the bottle of physic on the table. Puzzled and frightened, she looks at Jekyll, but he gives no sign. There is a pause, and then she quickly returns the bottle to the bureau. She turns round to see Jekyll still motionless

Good-night, sir. (*She bobs politely*)

Charlotte exits

Jekyll sits down and looks at the table. He relaxes as he sees that the bottle has gone

Jekyll Lottiekins—God bless you, Lottiekins. (*He calmly closes his notebook and returns it to the bureau*) Another day—but how many more? (*He goes towards the parlour door*)

The Lights fade to a Black-out. During the Black-out, Jekyll's pen and ink are returned to the bureau from the table

Another evening. The Lights come up on Celestine and Jekyll, standing tensely apart

Celestine (*after a tense pause*) There is nothing more to say then. You will not change your ways.
Jekyll I cannot. (*Then more calmly*) No. I will not.
Celestine So be it. (*Sincerely*) All I can say, Henry, is that I am very sorry. (*She goes to the door. She waits, then turns*)

Jekyll is like a steam boiler, every action of hers adding fuel to the fire

I shall stay in London for another week, if after that time I have not heard . . . (*She sees Jekyll's inner torment—she is frightened*) Henry.
Jekyll (*bursting out*) I must taste freedom again! Do you hear? I must breathe. You suffocate me. (*Earnestly*) Do not wait a week, Celestine. Go tonight— go now. (*He unlocks the laboratory door*) Go now do you hear me? Go!! (*He goes into the laboratory, slamming the door behind him*)

With affronted pride, Celestine goes to follow him, then changes her mind and goes to exit in the other direction, but her resolve gives way to fear and disappointment and she sinks slowly into the armchair, sobbing

During the next few speeches, Jekyll quietly exits from the laboratory. While off stage, he should apply his Hyde make-up

Charlotte enters, duster in hand

Charlotte Oh, sorry, madam. I didn't know anyone was here. (*She goes to exit*)
Celestine (*recovering but keeping her face turned away*) It's all right, I was just leaving.
Charlotte (*with a simple understanding*) Can I get you anything, madam?
Celestine (*rising*) Of course not. (*She has now regained her composure*)
Charlotte (*standing aside from the door*) Very good, madam.

Celestine (*genuinely*) Thank you for asking, Charlotte.

Celestine exits

Charlotte looks after her with a smile of sympathy, then busies herself dusting. She looks up as there is the sound of glass breaking in the laboratory, off

Hyde enters the laboratory and opens the door to the parlour

Charlotte Doctor, I . . . Ohhhhh! (*She backs away into the shadows*)

Hyde comes into the parlour, alive with evil glee

Hyde What a night—so much time to make up, he he, a nice night to make up time. (*He crosses to the sideboard and takes up a bottle of drink. He throws the stopper away*) A nice night for so many things. (*He takes a hefty drink, and again*)

In the shadows, Charlotte is trying to pluck up courage to face him

(*Lecherously*) So many things.

Charlotte comes into view

Well! here's a pretty little thing to start on. (*He drinks*) Ain't you, eh, gal. Ain't you! (*He grabs her*)

Charlotte Doctor said you might come. He gave me something for you. (*She manages to break away and gets the bottle of physic from the bureau*)

Hyde Did he now. That was nice of the doctor. (*He drinks*) Very nice. (*He puts the bottle down*) Let's see it. Come on little puss, let's see it. And let's see you.

She crosses to him. He grabs her wrist and looks at the physic she holds

Yes, that looks as if it would taste very nice. (*He takes it out of her hand*) But not as nice as you.

He throws away the physic and clasps Charlotte close to him, laughing in her face. She struggles then kicks him in the shin. His laughter turns to a roar and she breaks away. Hyde smiles evilly, drains his bottle, tosses it behind the armchair and crosses to Charlotte

Penny slips quietly into the laboratory

Charlotte (*desperately*) But you must take it.

Hyde (*advancing on her*) Don't you worry, little 'un. I'm going to.

He grabs her and carries her bodily into the centre of the room

(*Leching*) Oh yes. I'm going to take it.

The door of the laboratory behind him flies open and Penny stands there

Penny No you bleeding ain't.

Hyde drops Charlotte. She lies on the floor sobbing

I knew it, I knew it. I knew you were about here somewhere, and I knew what you were up to.

Hyde How the hell . . . ?
Penny I've been true to you. Cripes save I have. For the first time in my life
I wanted . . .
Hyde How did you get here?
Penny It ain't hard to pinch a key from you when you're slewed. I wanted
you, Edward Hyde, I would have done anything for you. But you went
away—you left me. I knew I shouldn't trust you, and now I hates you. Do
you hear? I hate you.
Hyde Ain't nice to hate a person.

Charlotte recovers enough to creep round and pick up the physic

Penny (*quietly*) I don't. I love you. But there is a great big hole in my heart—
and it's full up with hate. (*Violently*) You could have done bleeding better
than that though, couldn't you? Punch me, she's only a dolly-mop.
Hyde (*menacingly*) Stow it.
Penny A stinking little goose like that instead of me!
Hyde Stow it!!

Penny is about to continue. He lands her a back hander. Charlotte cuts in

Charlotte (*fearfully*) Leave her alone.

This stops his second blow

(*To Penny*) If you really loved him you'd try and help him. (*She indicates
the physic*)
Penny Love!? I'll scratch your ruddy eyes out.
Hyde (*really threateningly*) You dare! (*He comes between them*) Lottiekins
ain't done no harm.

*The mention of "Lottiekins" frightens Charlotte and raises an uncontrollable
fear in Hyde*

Penny What's up? Do you love her more than me? Do you! Answer me!!
Hyde Shut up. Shut up!
Penny You do—you bleeding do!
Hyde I don't—I can't! (*He is desperate, torn between two loves. His move-
ments are becoming uncontrolled. He lurches against the armchair and falls.
He picks up the false bottle from behind it*) How can I? I don't know her.
How can I know her?
Penny You love that little pudden.
Hyde (*standing up*) Shut up. Help me.
Penny (*viciously taunting him*) That—instead of me. After what I've meant
to you. You're mad—bleeding mad, that's what you are.
Hyde (*exploding*) Shut up!!
Penny No.

*Hyde swings the bottle to hit Penny. Charlotte tries to stop him by grabbing
his arm. He knocks her off and in a swift movement sweeps round and crashes
the bottle down on her head. It shatters. She falls behind the chair. There is
a shocked pause*

Penny You've done it now—my God you've done it.
Hyde Yes I have haven't I? She won't bother us any more Penny. (*He brings the bottle down again on the form behind the chair*)
Penny You've gone mad. (*She backs away*)
Hyde Not any more. (*He is alive with evil. The bottle crashes down again*)
Penny No—no. (*She backs away then turns and escapes through the laboratory door*)
Hyde Nobody will bother me any more.

As he rises, a picture of depravity, the Lights fade to a Black-out and—

the CURTAIN *falls*

SCENE 2

The same. Morning, a few days later

The Lights come up on both the parlour and laboratory. The curtains in the parlour are now open. Poole is standing by the closed laboratory door, looking rather fraught

Jekyll enters the laboratory from R, carrying a phial. He is distraught and dishevelled, with a hint of Hyde in his movements

Poole taps on the laboratory door, and calls through it

Poole Sir.
Jekyll Well, has it come?
Poole No, sir. Not yet. I wondered if there . . .
Jekyll For God's sake, Poole, how many more times!
Poole (*pained*) Sorry, sir.
Jekyll (*shuffling off*) There is only one thing that can help me now . . .

Jekyll exits R

Poole stands shaking his head for a moment, as the Lights fade on the laboratory

The parlour door opens and Hilda shows in Utterson, who is just getting over a very bad cold. Hilda retires immediately

Utterson Where the plague is everybody, Poole? (*He coughs and splutters*)
Poole I am glad you have called, sir. But you are not well.
Utterson Had a bout of fever—over it now. Had to come out or I swear that that damn'd Mrs Camp would have killed me with her cures. Fine thing when you have friends who are doctors and you can't find trace of them when you want them. Typical of damn'd medics though. Where is everybody, Poole? You look half dead yourself—what's happening?
Poole I wish to God I knew, sir.
Utterson (*sensing the tension*) Better tell me. (*He indicates that Poole should sit down*)

Poole (*sitting*) You have heard of the murder?

Utterson Who hasn't?

Poole There has been not sight nor sound of the villain since. Discharged his rooms in Soho, burnt all his papers and then vanished. People blame the master for trying to help Mr Hyde you know, sir.

Utterson I'm not surprised. What did Jekyll do?

Poole That is what is so strange, sir. For a few days the master was quite like his old self, very busy—out working—as if he—had come to a decision of some sort. But I am sure he was not well.

Utterson Oh?

Poole I noticed that he was taking physic, sir, quite regularly.

Utterson Where is he now?

Poole (*indicating the laboratory*) Where he has been for nigh on a week now, sir. Ever since last—Friday it must have been. (*He pauses*) It was cold and fine, in the morning; the master came downstairs, he looked calm and relaxed. I must have shown my feelings because—I remember the exact words—he said, "Don't look so surprised, Poole, I am only going out for a walk, just a walk." He has not spoken to me calmly since. (*He pauses, the retelling breaking down his reserve*)

Utterson waits patiently

I heard nothing more that day until early evening when a boy brought a note in the master's hand. It said that Dr Lanyon would call and that I was to allow him into the laboratory. I knew there was something wrong but there was nothing I could do. Almost immediately the doctor arrived, he had a similar note with instructions to collect certain compounds; I do not know what, I was ordered to stay outside.

Utterson (*prompting*) Did he take them?

Poole Yes sir, very mysterious about it all he was. The master must have returned during the night, and he has been in—there!—ever since.

Utterson Um. Doesn't he say anything at all?

Poole The only messages we get are orders for chemicals, usually the same chemical, to be fetched from various suppliers, he never seems satisfied. The last one was right down in Tilbury, if you please. What am I to do, sir?

Utterson Don't know. Better go and see Lanyon, see what he has to say. (*He turns towards the parlour door*)

The door opens and Celestine is shown in by Hilda

Celestine There is no need, Mr Utterson. Dr Lanyon has come round to speak for himself. (*To Hilda*) Would you be kind enough to see if you can help my uncle.

Hilda exits

Gentlemen, I must speak before my uncle comes. To prepare you, gentlemen . . . My uncle is dying. (*Ignoring their reactions*) Yes dying. (*Trying to retain her composure*) I implored him not to but he insisted on coming here. (*To Utterson*) I am so glad you are here. I just cannot understand it—it is as if some devil has taken his will to live.

Utterson How long has he been like this?
Celestine Since Saturday morning. Something has broken his spirit. I . . .

The door opens and Hilda helps in a pathetic shadow of the previous Lanyon

The others help him into a chair. Hilda turns to go but Celestine signs that she would like her to stay. Lanyon sits trembling. The others wait. Celestine kneels at his side

Uncle—Mr Utterson is here.
Lanyon (*turning to look at him slowly*) Good of you to come, Utterson. (*After a pause*) I've seen the Devil. I've met Lucifer face to face. God is not a person on this earth, but the Devil is. I cannot stay where God is not. I have called the Devil my friend! (*He fidgets with his gloves*)

Utterson gives Celestine a look of pained disbelief, and she nods sadly. Lanyon drops one of his gloves on the floor. Hilda picks it up and as she places it in his lap, Lanyon takes her hand. He seems to find comfort from her hand; Hilda does not know what to do. Celestine indicates to her that she should stay there, and Hilda kneels by the chair

There is little warmth in the world. This hand is warm.
Hilda What does evil look like, sir?
Lanyon Like Dr Jekyll, that is what the Devil is like. When he is not being a murderer! (*He calms down a little and continues, becoming more lucid and composed as he relates his story*) Until last week my faith protected me. But my own conceit stripped it away last Friday night. A boy brought me a note from Henry telling me to come here to the laboratory and take a bottle of physic. Just one bottle that was locked away; and I was to give it to whoever should ask for it at twelve o'clock at my house that night. I did as I was bid. At midnight to the minute a figure entered through the door that I had left open. It shambled in keeping away from the light, but its eyes seemed to glow—like coals of hell. I am not easily scared but that creature seemed to surround itself with a cold pool of pure hatred. Its face was contorted with both fear and ecstasy. "Have you got it?" he cried. "Have you got it?" He reached out and touched me, an icy pang ran along my blood. I drew back—"It's there", I said. He fell upon it—then turned and looked upon me with an air of scrutiny. "And now," he said, "will you be wise, will you suffer me to take this glass and go from your house— or has the greed of curiosity too much command of you?" If only I had said "Go you Devil—go!" (*He suddenly becomes agitated*)
Celestine Uncle . . .
Lanyon (*in a world of his own*) Twice he asked me and twice I said "Proceed, sir." "What you believe will be lost to you," he said, "and what you have refused to accept you must now believe—behold!" (*He re-lives his narrative*) As he drank he was seized by a dreadful spasm. That vile face contorted and twisted—I could not bear the sight. But I couldn't turn away. "Oh God", I cried. Was this human? Was it real? His whole body was changing. "Oh God. Oh God." Before my eyes this creature shuddered into a different shape. "God, no!" There before me stood my life-long friend Dr Henry

Jekyll. He and this satanic monster were the same thing. Oh God—oh
God—oh God ... (*He collapses back in the chair*)

The others move in to him as the Lights cross-fade to the laboratory

*Jekyll enters the laboratory from R, carrying two bottles, one of which is
almost empty, and goes to the workbench*

Jekyll They look alike—by Hades, they must be the same this time. Same
ingredients, same procedure. I must find out. (*He puts down the almost empty
bottle and pours a small quantity of the other into a glass*) I must risk it.
If he comes—(*looking at the bottle*)—then it works and he can go. (*He drinks.
Waits. Nothing*) Hades! (*He takes a drink from the bottle*) It could be water!
(*His control is nearly breaking. He throws the bottle away. Calming down
a little, he takes up the almost empty bottle*) Only two left. Pray God—will
they be enough ... (*He puts the bottle down very carefully*) Must not sleep.
He hovers like a shadow—he comes in sleep, must not sleep. (*He takes up
his notebook and pen and sits on the arm of the chair. Writing*) "Completed
new mix of F.M. with fresh supply crystals. Fourth failure. Is God the
master of science after all? Eternity is near ..." (*He stops writing and slips
into the chair*)

*The Lights cross-fade to the parlour. Jekyll should apply his Hyde make-up dur-
ing the next few speeches, while the laboratory is in darkness*

Hilda and Utterson are helping Lanyon to his feet

Celestine I know, but we must get him away from here, away from that place.
(*She looks towards the laboratory*)
Poole You'll come back, sir?
Utterson Naturally.
Celestine (*moving to help Hilda with Lanyon*) Thank you my dear, we'll
manage between us. (*To Poole*) I'll not keep her long.

*Celestine gives a long look at the laboratory door, then she, Utterson and Hilda
exit with Lanyon*

There is a pause

Hilda (*off*) There is a packet come for the doctor, Mr Poole.
Poole I'll take it.

*Poole exits and returns quickly with a small poison bottle and a packet. He
reads "L-e-t-a-l-i-s" from the label on the bottle and then puts both by the
laboratory door and exits L again*

The Lights cross-fade to the laboratory. Jekyll/Hyde is asleep in the chair

Jekyll (*shouting in his sleep*) Lottiekins! Go away Lottiekins. (*He wakes up*)
Lottie ... What? Must not sleep. (*He rises, keeping his back to the audience*)
Thank God. Thank God he didn't come. (*He wearily goes to the door unlocks
and opens it. His voice and deportment are Jekyll's but as he looks through
the door to the parlour, the audience will see that his face is Hyde's. He picks
up the bottle and packet left by Poole and returns to the laboratory, locking

the door behind him. His personality is now in balance, and in the following speeches, he alternates between Jekyll and Hyde) Must not give up. *(Indicating the packet)* This must do it. Then ever smaller doses—that must be the way.

Hyde *(with a sudden sneering laugh)* No!

Jekyll That must be the way. God, I can't think. *(He clears the things off the stool with a clatter and puts the bottle and packet down. He notices that one of the things he has knocked off the stool is a mirror. He picks it up carefully, afraid to look in it. Eventually he does)*

Hyde *(laughing again)* Who did you expect to see?

Jekyll I don't know. *(He takes up the packet)* I can hold you at bay long enough to make a new batch. This is from the same source as the original, it must . . . it must . . . *(Desperately)* It won't! *(He throws the packet down)*

He now begins to alternate between Jekyll and Hyde. As he stumbles about he alternates between laughing as Hyde, and calling out "It won't!" and "Go . . . go . . . no!" as Jekyll. He grabs the bottle, knocking over the stool. Holding the bottle up, he screams out "Go to hell!" and then seems to calm down

That may not work but you will. You will work very well. Why? Why? Why? The procedure—the mixture—the compound—all the same. *(Beginning to see)* Of course, they are right—it was the original that was wrong. That original batch of crystals was . . . *(He puts down the bottle, calmer but very, very weary. He picks up his notebook and tries to write)* "Clearly some impurity in the first batch was the key; nature unknown." I have succeeded—I have failed. I am lost, I can fight no more. *(He sits with his head in his hands)*

Hyde *(chuckling)* That's nice, that's very nice.

The Lights cross-fade to the parlour

Poole enters, goes to the bookcase and removes a book. He opens the book and looks through it

Utterson enters

Utterson Poor girl, her life has collapsed about her.

Poole Haven't all our lives?

Utterson What are you looking up?

Poole Letalis.

Utterson What do you want to know that for? It's Latin. It means death.

Poole *(putting the book down and looking at the laboratory)* We must do something.

Utterson Got to get them out of there, that's the first thing.

Poole Him! It's only the master.

Utterson Him—them. How? That room's built like a fortress.

There is a knock at the parlour door

Poole Yes.

Penny *(off)* It's all right, I know the way.

Penny enters

Utterson Who the devil is this?

Penny I could say the same.

Poole It's Hyde's woman, sir. I'd forgotten I'd sent for her, when I thought Hyde was locked in there . . .

Utterson He is.

Poole I—well, I had some idea she might—entice him out.

Utterson She might still do that.

Penny Here. What's going on? Who's enticing who?

Utterson Mr Hyde has locked himself in that room. He is in need of help. We think you may be able to get him to come out.

Penny So that you can help him.

Utterson Yes.

Penny And if I don't?

Utterson Then we think he will die.

Penny So if I get him to come out you can help him—and if I don't he will die.

Utterson Yes.

Penny Then it looks as if he will die, doesn't it?

Poole I thought you were supposed to love him, and he love you. Where is this great bond that you were so full of?

Penny How the hell did you know anything about that?

Poole Never mind how I know. If you loved him you would help him—whatever he has done.

Penny You people make me sick. "If you really loved him." Of course I really loved him; with my whole body I really loved him, and he loved me, by God.

Utterson Then you will help?

Penny just looks at him

Why not?

Penny 'Cause when you are like us there is only one sort of love you can afford. And that takes two people. Well, there ain't bleeding well two people now, are there? One of them is in there, and he is as good as dead. If you don't kill him then Jack Ketch will. That's why you will have to get him out yourselves. (*She takes a large key from her pocket and begins to fidget with it as she talks*)

Celestine quietly enters

(*With bitter calmness*) My sort ain't allowed to love with the head—or the heart—only the guts. Don't you understand? Now there's no way for me to love. My love is dead. I can't help you. (*She turns to go and comes face to face with Celestine. After a pause*) And I wouldn't bleeding well help you if I could!

Penny throws down the key and runs out, almost in tears

Celestine bends down and picks up the key. Utterson looks at her questioningly

Celestine (*nodding sadly*) I have sent Hilda . . .

Utterson (*going to her*) I think I'd better take you . . .

Celestine No, I must not give way. I have returned because—while Henry is alive—(*with a sad smile*)—I am allowed to love him with my head it seems. (*Almost breaking down*) Although any other way is going to be denied me, I fear.

Poole Madam. Excuse me. (*He takes the key she is holding*) It's the same as the one that came from Mr Monk. (*To Utterson*) Sir—the mews door— we can get to him.

Poole exits

Utterson goes to follow him then turns to Celestine

Utterson Stay here my dear . . .

Celestine I am coming with you.

Celestine exits determinedly, Utterson following her

The Lights cross-fade to the laboratory. Hyde sits on the chair, singing drunkenly. This gives way to quiet laughter

Hyde Yes. That's the way, I can manage that. They won't catch Edward Hyde. Not clever Mr Edward Hyde. (*He sings a few more bars*) I've been too clever haven't I? (*He stops suddenly and swings round*) Who's there? Come on, who's there I say?

Charlotte's Voice (*very quietly*) It's me, sir.

Hyde's bravado changes to fear, he cannot see her

Hyde No, no. It can't be. Not you. Can't be you because you're dead—(*He sees what he thinks is her up in the shadows*) No . . . Go away, do you hear. Leave me alone. (*He turns away*) I didn't mean to kill you—didn't want to kill you. I liked you really—pity you had to be the one. Couldn't help it. Can't help being what I am. (*He turns back, he can still see her*) For God's sake—what do you want? What have you come for? Don't just stand there! Streuth! What can I do?

Charlotte's Voice It's Lottiekins, sir.

The name affects him

Little Lottiekins, sir.

Hyde Lottiekins—I don't know no Lottiekins—go away Lottiekins.

He keeps repeating "Lottiekins" and "Go away Lottiekins", his voice changing from Hyde to Jekyll, until Jekyll's voice is constant

Jekyll (*looking round, more composed*) I can't see you, Lottiekins. Where . . . ? Must hold on, must try to hold on. (*He goes to the workbench and stands in front of the two bottles, one of poison and the almost empty one*) Must try to hold on long enough, Lottiekins. (*With shaking hands he opens the almost empty bottle*) Long enough. (*His face suddenly contorts*)

Hyde lets out a roar

Hyde I can bloody well see you. I know what you are up to! (*He crashes the bottle to the ground and laughs with glee*) There it's gone! Gone!! (*He rampages about. He takes up the notebook, his eyes alight, and tears out the pages. Calling*) Gone! Gone! Gone! (*Delighted, he looks around*) Gone. Everything's gone. Dr Jekyll, gone! Gone. (*He rests on the chair, breathless*) I'm too clever by far. Lottiekins can't do it—no-one can do it. I've beaten them—'cause I'm Edward Hyde. Edward Hyde. (*He lapses into a breathless silence*)

Poole, Utterson and Celestine enter the laboratory from R

How the hell! Get! Do you hear? Out! Or I'll . . .
Poole (*coming forward*) I'll help you, sir, it's all right . . .

With one swing Hyde floors Poole. As he turns to look for a suitable weapon, the others help Poole to get out of his way. Hyde grabs a bottle or the stool and turns threateningly. Celestine stands calmly before him

Celestine Well, Henry—are you going to kill me too? Henry?

Hyde wants to strike but some power seems to prevent him

Hyde Not Henry. I'm not Henry.
Celestine I don't think I mind if you do kill me. My uncle is dead. My future is dead. Henry. (*She stands looking straight at him*)

There is a long pause, then suddenly Hyde slowly turns to the bench, takes up the poison bottle and drinks. Celestine moves forward instinctively, but Utterson restrains her. Nothing happens for a moment then a convulsion seizes Hyde. Without a sound, he staggers to the chair in agony and collapses. He lies there moaning. Utterson unlocks the laboratory door, and he and Celestine, unable to stand it, pass into the parlour. Hyde moans again, then staggers to his feet and turns to the front. He is Jekyll again. He falls dead to the floor. Poole stands loyally looking at his master, then bends and closes his eyes. He picks up the notebook and torn pages and passes into the parlour

The Lights cross-fade to the parlour. Celestine is sitting in the armchair being comforted by Hilda. Poole gives the bundle of paper to Utterson

Utterson The kitchen fire is well alight, is it not?
Hilda Oh yes, sir. (*She goes to take the papers*)
Utterson No. I will do it.

Utterson exits L

Celestine sits crying quietly, comforted by Hilda. Poole stands looking into the laboratory as the Lights fade to a Black-out and—

the CURTAIN *falls*

FURNITURE AND PROPERTY LIST

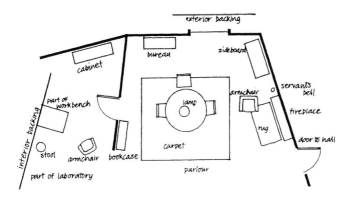

ACT I

PARLOUR:
Table. *On it:* chenille tablecloth, lamp (practical)
3 upright chairs
Armchair. *Hidden behind it:* make-up, wig etc. for **Jekyll** to
become **Hyde**
Sideboard. *On it:* tantalus with decanters of claret, Madeira
($\frac{1}{4}$ full) and brandy ($\frac{1}{2}$ full), glasses, jug of water, tray, other
bottles of drink.
Bureau. *On it:* pens, bottles of ink. *In drawer* (practical lock):
notebook
Bookcase. *On shelves:* books
Window curtains (open)
Carpet
In front of fireplace: rug
On mantelpiece: box of matches, candlestick
On wall: servant's bell

LABORATORY:
Armchair
Workbench. *On it:* lamp (not practical); phials, measuring
glasses, mixing rods, dishes, tweezers and other apparatus;
wooden carrying case containing various jars and bottles
(one wrapped); doctor's bag.

Cabinet. *On shelves*: bottles and jars of chemicals
Stool. *On it*: various books, mirror
In door to parlour: key

Off stage: Duster (**Charlotte**)
                Package containing phial of crystals (**Poole**)

Personal   **Jekyll**: pocket-watch
                Jekyll: small key for bureau drawer
                Utterson: cigars
                Utterson: cigar-trimmer

SCENE 2

Strike: Dirty glasses

Reset: **Jekyll's** apparatus on bench in laboratory
                Notebook, pen and ink in bureau
                Window curtains open
                Doors closed

Set: Bucket. *In it*: coal
                Coal glove
                Cleaning materials (dusters, polish, brooms etc.)

Off stage: Key (**Poole**)
                Bowl of water and cloth (Hilda)

Personal: **Jekyll**: key for laboratory
                Jekyll: small key for bureau drawer
                Jekyll: envelope containing will

SCENE 3

Strike: Bowl of water
                Cloth

Reset: Lamp on sideboard
                Doors closed

Set: On table: white tablecloth, 2 dirty plates with cutlery, 2 wine
                    glasses, 2 dessert spoons, cruet, 2 napkins.
                Under table: **Hyde** make-up
                On sideboard: decanter of wine, 2 glasses of syllabub 2 trays
                    (for **Hilda** and **Charlotte**)

Off stage: Tray. *On it*: teapot, 2 cups and saucers, teaspoons, milk-jug,
                    sugar bowl (**Hilda**)
                Tray (**Charlotte**)

Personal: **Jekyll**: key for laboratory door

ACT II

SCENE 1

Strike: Key from floor
                Jekyll's bag from table
                Dirty glass

Reset: Lamp on table

Set: *Behind armchair*: trick bottle (for **Hyde**)
               On workbench in laboratory: small bottle of physic

Off stage: Bag (**Jekyll**)
               Tray. *On it*: plate of food, glass of ale, cutlery (**Charlotte**)
               Tablecloth (**Hilda**)
               Tray. *On it*: plate, cutlery, cruet, napkin, dishes of food (**Charlotte**)
               Duster (**Charlotte**)

Personal: **Jekyll**: key for laboratory door

SCENE 2

Strike: Broken bottle
               Empty bottle
               Bottle of physic

Reset: Window curtains open
               Doors closed
               Notebook, pen and ink in laboratory

Set: Laboratory
               In door to parlour: key
               Beside armchair (concealed): **Hyde** make-up

Off stage: Phial (**Jekyll**)
               2 bottles of liquid, one almost empty (**Jekyll**)
               Small poison bottle labelled "Letalis" (**Poole**)
               Small packet (**Poole**)

Personal: **Lanyon**: gloves
               Penny: key

LIGHTING PLOT

Practical fittings required: lamp
Interior. A parlour and part of the adjoining laboratory. The same scene throughout

ACT I Scene 1. Early evening

To open:	Effect of early evening light in parlour. Laboratory dimmed	
Cue 1	**Utterson** trims cigar in fireplace	(Page 10)
	Start slow fade of early evening light to give effect of dusk falling	
Cue 2	**Poole** lights lamp	(Page 14)
	Bring up lamp and covering spot on table	

ACT I Scene 2. Morning

To open:	Effect of daylight in parlour. Laboratory dimmed	
Cue 3	**Jekyll** tends to the **Child**	(Page 28)
	Fade to Black-out	

ACT I Scene 3. Afternoon

To open:	Effect of daylight in parlour. Laboratory dimmed	
Cue 4	**Hyde**: ". . . Not nice at all."	(Page 39)
	Fade to Black-out	

ACT II Scene 1. Evening

To open:	Effect of dim evening light in parlour; lamp lit, turned down low. Laboratory dimmed	
Cue 5	**Jekyll** turns up lamp	(Page 40)
	Increase lamp and covering spot on table	
Cue 6	**Jekyll** turns down lamp	(Page 41)
	Fade lamp and covering spot	
Cue 7	**Jekyll** exits	(Page 41)
	Black-out	
Cue 8	When ready	(Page 42)
	Bring up general lighting in parlour to give effect of dull daylight	
Cue 9	**Jekyll**: "My own devices—ha!"	(Page 45)
	Fade to Black-out	
Cue 10	When ready	(Page 45)
	Bring up dim overall lighting in parlour, lamp and covering spot	
Cue 11	**Jekyll**: " . . . but how many more?"	(Page 46)
	Fade to Black-out	

Cue 12	When ready	(Page 46)
	Repeat Cue 10	
Cue 13	**Hyde:** " . . . bother me any more."	(Page 49)
	Fade to Black-out	

ACT II Scene 2. Morning

To open:	Effect of daylight in parlour and laboratory	
Cue 14	**Jekyll** exits R from laboratory	(Page 49)
	Fade Lights on laboratory	
Cue 15	**Lanyon** collapses back in chair	(Page 52)
	Cross-fade to laboratory	
Cue 16	**Jekyll** sits in armchair	(Page 52)
	Cross-fade to parlour	
Cue 17	**Poole** exits	(Page 52)
	Cross-fade to laboratory	
Cue 18	**Hyde:** " . . . that's very nice."	(Page 53)
	Cross-fade to parlour	
Cue 19	**Celestine** and **Utterson** exit L	(Page 55)
	Cross-fade to laboratory	
Cue 20	**Poole** picks up notebook and goes through into parlour	(Page 56)
	Cross-fade to parlour	
Cue 21	**Utterson** exits L with notebook	(Page 56)
	Slowly fade to Black-out	

EFFECTS PLOT

ACT I

Cue 1	**Charlotte**: "Perhaps he's ill." *Clatter of bucket being knocked over off L*	(Page 18)
Cue 2	**Hilda**: " . . . go right through the floor." *Clatter of bucket being knocked over off L*	(Page 19)
Cue 3	**Hilda** exits with cleaning materials *Clatter off L*	(Page 20)
Cue 4	**Jekyll** exits R from laboratory *Pause, then door slam off R*	(Page 25)

ACT II

Cue 5	**Celestine** exits and **Charlotte** dusts *Sound of breaking glass in laboratory off L*	(Page 47)

Lightning Source UK Ltd.
Milton Keynes UK
UKOW031217200513

210956UK00005B/22/P